THE ANCIENT OLYMPICS

THE ANCIENT OLYMPICS

NIGEL SPIVEY

OXFORD
UNIVERSITY PRESS

OXFORD
UNIVERSITY PRESS

Great Clarendon Street, Oxford OX2 6DP

Oxford University Press is a department of the University of Oxford.
It furthers the University's objective of excellence in research, scholarship,
and education by publishing worldwide in

Oxford New York

Auckland Bangkok Buenos Aires Cape Town Chennai
Dar es Salaam Delhi Hong Kong Istanbul Karachi Kolkata
Kuala Lumpur Madrid Melbourne Mexico City Mumbai Nairobi
São Paulo Shanghai Taipei Tokyo Toronto

Oxford is a registered trade mark of Oxford University Press
in the UK and in certain other countries

Published in the United States
by Oxford University Press Inc., New York

British Library Cataloguing in Publication Data
Data applied for

Library of Congress Cataloging in Publication Data
Data available

ISBN 0-19-280433-2

I

Printed in Great Britain by
Clays Ltd, St Ives plc

CONTENTS

LIST OF ILLUSTRATIONS

1. Panorama of Olympia © Yann Arthus-Bertrand/Corbis

2. Fragment of an Athenian black-figure bowl showing chariots and crowds at the 'games of Patroklos': National Archaeological Museum, Athens, inv. 15499. Photo: © TAP Service, NAM, Athens

3. Gymnasium at Delphi © Alinari Archives, Florence

4. Plunge bath at Delphi © Professor Stephen G. Miller

5. *Palaistra* at Olympia, with plan © Ancient Art & Architecture Collection

6. Bronze figure of an *Apoxyomenos* ('scraper'): Croatian Conservation Institute, Zagreb. Photo: © Vidoslav Barac/CCI

7. Courtship scene on an Athenian black-figure amphora: Staatliche Antikensammlungen, Munich, inv. 1468. Photo: © Koppermann/SAM

8. Marble torso after the Polykleitan 'Discophorus': The J. Paul Getty Museum, Malibu, California, inv. 79.AA.146. Photo: © J. Paul Getty Museum

9. Red-figured Athenian drinking cup showing athletes of various body shapes: British Museum, inv. E6. Photo: © The British Museum

10. Roman marble copy of the Doryphoros ('Spear-Carrier') by Polykleitos: National Archaeological Museum, Naples. Photo: © Alinari Archives, Florence

ACKNOWLEDGEMENTS

Given the institutional longevity and centrality of Olympia throughout Classical times, the history of the ancient Olympics is surprisingly uncertain in many details. I have tried to indicate areas of doubt and disagreement in the course of the text; and have been saved from sheer error by colleagues whose advice I have gratefully used. In particular, Paul Cartledge and Don Kyle each read and corrected drafts of the book; Anthony Snodgrass helped with Chapter 6, and Malcolm Willcock assisted with Pindar.

KEY TO ABBREVIATIONS

FrGrH: F. Jacoby, *Die Fragmente der griechischen Historiker* (Berlin, 1923–).

IG: *Inscriptiones Graecae*.

IvO: W. Dittenberger and K. Purgold, *Die Inschriften von Olympia* (Berlin, 1896).

SEG: *Supplementum Epigraphicum Graecum*.

OLYMPIA AND THE CLASSICAL WORLD

0	250	500	750 km
0		250	500 miles

ETRURIA

ADRIATIC SEA

CORSICA

Rome

MACEDONIA
Mt. Olympus ▲

Olympia

SARDINIA

MAGNA
GRECIA

Metapontion

Croton

Motya

SICILY

Rhegion

Carthage

Akragas

Gela

Syracuse

M E D I T E R R

Dodona
thessaly

Corfu

Pergamon

lydia

ithaca

Delphi

Thebes

Euboea

▲ Mt. Sipylos

Elis
Sikyon
Nemea

Megara
Marathon
Athens

Samos

Ephesos

Olympia

Mycenae

Corinth

Miletus

Argos
Tiryns

Aegina

caria

Cyrene

Messene

Epidauros

Delos

Pylos

Sparta

Naxos

Kos

Thera

Rhodes

Crete

Knossos

0	50	100	150 km
0		50	100 miles

OVERTURE

We arrive in coachloads. Yet Olympia today still strikes us as a site of marvellous seclusion and natural tranquillity (Fig. 1). Every variegation of green appears to flourish here. Oak and olive, cypress and citrus – this is a landscape that settles the soul. The ruins lie low, as if organically belonging to the fertile course of the River Alpheios. The Alpheios itself, fringed by willows and the gentle hubbub of bamboo, flows easy and broad, with relaxed eddies around gravel islands. Earthquakes and torrents seem unimaginable in this part of the world.

The peace is an illusion. Cataclysm has visited Olympia more than once in the past. And if we had come to the sanctuary when its structures stood their ground, we should probably not have liked it much. For one thing, Olympia was just that: a sanctuary, where many strange deities were worshipped in ways that would surely disgust us. Supreme among these deities was Zeus. His shrine lay in a leafy grove at the foot of a small forested hill. But that was the extent of its pastoral calm. Oxen were brought in by the hundred to be sacrificed to the god: their bellowings resounded down

1.   Panorama of Olympia.

the valley as they were axed before a crowd, and the precincts steeped black with their blood. Ash, bones, and bovine offal piled up over centuries into a huge pyramid: it must have reeked to high heaven.

Could we have endured this for the sake of Olympia's pride: the great, original 'Olympic Games'? Again, it is doubtful. Much human blood was spilled here too. The most esteemed contestants at these so-called 'Games' were all-in fighters to whom bruises meant little – athletes whose victories came at the cost of their blood, teeth, looks, and consciousness – while the main spectacle was a challenge far too hazardous ever to figure in the modern Olympic programme. Chariot-racing was packed with risks to life and limb. Its protagonists could feel deeply grateful just to reach the finishing-post in one piece.

The festival was noisy – especially after 396 BC, when contests for heralds and trumpet-blowers were introduced. It was also hideously congested, and for hundreds of years deprived of adequate accommodation, water supply, and sanitation; not to mention marred by the standard plagues of heat, flies, and hucksters. Anyone with something to sell or publicize was liable to turn up at Olympia: flagrant exhibitionism was not confined to the (stark naked) male athletes. Poets and painters would strut about in gaudy robes, astronomers display their latest calculations about the cosmos. Philosophers made extraordinary appearances. The sixth-century BC guru Pythagoras, for example, came over from Croton – a city with a reputation for producing successful athletes – and added to his own enigmatic cult status by revealing to spectators in the Stadium at Olympia that one of his thighs was made of gold. In the fifth century BC, the travelling intellectuals known as Sophists also featured at the festival. One of their specialities was demonstrating the sort of combative oratory suited to assemblies and law courts: so they put on shows of such verbal dexterity and aggression in front of Olympic crowds.

We could go on. The point is that the ruins of ancient Olympia are deceptively quiet, and should not be idealized with too much faded grandeur. The return of the modern Olympics to Greece in 2004 may be glossed with some sentiment of spiritual homecoming, but it is hardly an accurate simulation of antiquity – a mercy for which we may be truly thankful. Our own Olympic tradition began in 1896. While some aspects of the modern jamboree may now curiously reflect ancient conditions – the hucksters, certainly; also the intensely specialized preparation of the athletes – it is safe to say that Olympia past is another country; 'sport' was done differently there.

This book is a journey to the strangeness, the historical particularities, of that place.

Some modern sociologists would say that sport essentially functions as a sublimation or repression of violence. There was no such theorizing in antiquity, but we can trace plenty of evidence to prove an original purpose of Greek athletics as the *imitation* or *enactment* of violence. It is still possible to speak of the brutality of the ancient Olympics, even enumerate fatalities incurred during contest. But, as Chapter 1 elucidates, this understanding of sport as 'war minus the shooting' was profoundly civilized (and the fatalities at Olympia, over centuries of keen competition, remarkably few).

The civil or civic basis of ancient athletics is the subject of Chapter 2, which visits the world of the gymnasium as the Greeks conceived it. This shows us athletics as part of the daily routines of 'the care of the self' – such activities as washing, eating, sex, and sleep. Strenuous exercise was not only prescribed as a civic duty; the well-exercised body also became the subject of erotic and aesthetic interest, combining to shape the classical definition of *kalokagathia*, 'beautiful goodness'.

With Chapter 3 we arrive at Olympia – via the circuit of other 'All-Greek', or Panhellenic, Games. The astonishing fact is that not only were the ancient Olympics held every four years for an uninterrupted span of nearly 1,200 years, but their programme remained more or less unaltered over that time. 'All things are in flux', goes the saying of the Greek philosopher Herakleitos. But in terms of what athletes were expected to do, Olympia was like an island of stable conduct and established rules; a sanctuary whose very conservatism preserved its enduring *kudos* or renown around the Mediterranean.

Participation in these Games was not, emphatically,

about taking part; rather, athletes came to Olympia driven by an intense desire to win, to be recognized as the best. The keeping of a victory register that eventually became a mode of chronology in the Greek and Roman world did, quite literally, write winners into history. But Chapter 4 describes the further and more florid commemoration of athletic success in poetry and statues.

Chapter 5 is a necessary corrective to the often-voiced opinion that sport and politics are intrinsically separate. It follows the political history of Olympia from 776 BC to the official closure of the site *c*.AD 393.

Chapter 6 then tries to match the findings of modern archaeology with the mythical substrata of Olympia's origins. Perhaps it is as well to issue a warning at this juncture, however – to the effect that we must accept much of Olympia's literary history as already tinctured with myth.

Finally, in the brief postscript that is Chapter 7, we shall admit to our own making of myths: in particular, the well-meaning distortion of antiquity that propelled Pierre de Coubertin to 'revive' the Olympic Games as an international celebration of peace, goodwill, and athletic amateurism.

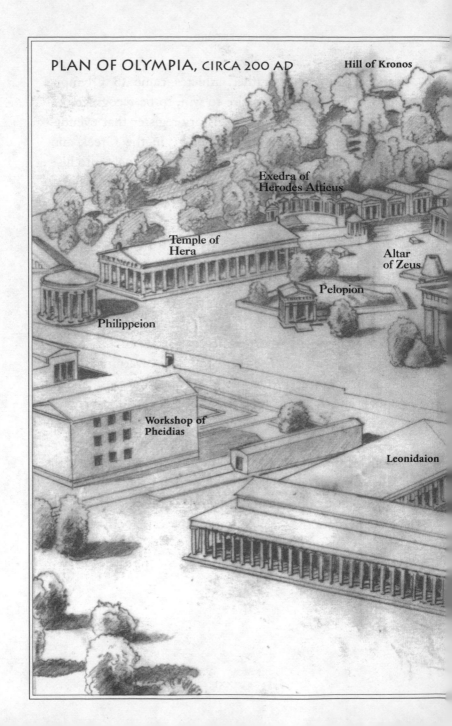

PLAN OF OLYMPIA, CIRCA 200 AD

Hill of Kronos

Exedra of
Herodes Atticus

Temple of
Hera

Altar
of Zeus

Pelopion

Philippeion

Workshop of
Pheidias

Leonidaion

1

'WAR MINUS THE SHOOTING'

Late in 1945 the English writer George Orwell turned his journalistic attention to the phenomenon of international soccer. The Second World War had ended with formal peace agreements in the summer of that year. As part of a return to normality, and in the spirit of fostering future concord, the Soviet Union had sent one of its leading football clubs, the Moscow Dynamos, on a round of 'friendly' fixtures with teams in Britain.

The encounters were, it seems, far from friendly. Players came to blows during the match with London's Arsenal, and huge crowds booed the referee. At Glasgow, the game pitched into a free-for-all. The Russians made protests about unfairness of team selection, and abandoned the tour prematurely. As Orwell observed: if this visit had any effect on Anglo-Soviet relations, it 'will have been to create fresh animosity on both sides'.

Typifying all international sporting contests as 'orgies of hatred', Orwell went on even to deny the cherished British virtue of gentlemanly conduct in sport. *'Serious sport,'* he ruled, *'has nothing to do with fair play. It is bound up with hatred, jealousy, boastfulness, disregard of all rules and sadistic pleasure in witnessing violence: in other words it is war minus the shooting.'*

This is overstatement – befitting the newspaper opinion column for which it was written. Nor, perhaps, is it much of a revelation. Orwell spent his formative years at Eton, the elite all-boys' college with a centuries-old tradition of insisting pupils take lessons in elegant attire, then letting them loose for pure rough-and-tumble in the mud. So, of his conclusive showdown with Napoleon Buonaparte in 1815, the Duke of Wellington – another old Etonian – might well have said that 'the battle of Waterloo was won on the playing fields of Eton': meaning, presumably, that the diehard ferocity and team spirit of his officers had been instilled by the primal rucks and tussles of England's most aristocratic public school.

'War minus the shooting' remains a neat epigram to the sentiment that sport is ultimately, or basically, a sublimated form of human aggression, a channelling of the biological instinct to fight. Popularized in the last century by the likes of Konrad Lorenz and Desmond Morris, this view may not claim the support of all behavioural psychologists today. But it remains tempting to explain the rituals of individual and team sports in the metaphoric terms of mock-combat − along with the pseudo-tribal antics of spectators. And Orwell's phrase seems especially apt for application to ancient Olympia, where war's encroachment upon athletic activity was overt and frequent. Quite apart from the fact that control of the sanctuary and its lucrative festival was several times the cause of war, and the sacred precincts on at least one occasion a battleground, the whole site, including the Stadium, was decked with spoils of armed conflict. Altars were attended by specialists in sacrosanct military intelligence; events were contested to the point of serious injury and fatality; and the entire programme of athletic 'games' could be rationalized as a set of drills for cavalry and infantry fighting.

It is not clear from Orwell's comments whether he sought to praise or to denounce sport's more or less latent aggression. If denunciation were intended, the obvious riposte is that war minus the shooting is surely preferable to war with the shooting. That, in fact, is rather how the Greeks came to justify and rationalize their Olympic and other Panhellenic contests. Neither the Greeks nor the Romans nursed any ideal concept of sport and recreation as a defining aspect of the human species: *Homo Ludens*, 'Man the Player', may be a Latin title, but it has nothing to do with Classical antiquity. Instead, there was an acceptance, at both popular and philosophical levels, of a prime imaginative and imitative purpose in play; an understanding, essentially, that all games were war games.

To put it another way: if George Orwell could have communed with fifth-century BC Athens and shared his observations about sport with Socrates, the local reaction is predictable: 'War minus the shooting'? Of course! What else would it be?

But this is a crude summary of ancient thinking, which deserves further exploration.

Bad Strife, Good Strife

It was one of the earliest surviving Greek poets, Hesiod, composing his verses probably around 700 BC, who not only made 'Strife' (*Eris*) a supernatural force to be reckoned with, but also divided this force into one Strife that was useful and productive (*Eris agathos*) and another that caused nothing but grief for humankind. This malevolent Strife, 'exulting in bad things' (*kakochartos*), was the bringer of war and dissent to the world. Good Strife, born of a coupling between Zeus and the Night, encouraged mortals to make the most of their brief time on earth; Bad Strife set up lusts for battle and bloodshed. Good Strife nurtured desires for wealth and fame; Bad Strife was a destroyer of lives and property. Good Strife urged creative industry, stirring the energies of emulation. So craftsmen competed amongst themselves, so farmers toiled to get the best from their land, so even beggars vied in their begging, and poets challenged other poets.

Hesiod's dual characterization of Strife comes in the opening passages of a didactic poem, the *Works and*

Days, ostensibly addressed to a brother who is inclined to be idle and heedless of Good Strife. Hesiod himself is glad to add the weight of personal experience to his proverbial advice. Once, he relates, he ventured across to Euboea and joined a rhapsodes' contest on the occasion of games held in honour of the hero Amphidamas. 'I was victorious with my song,' boasts Hesiod, 'I won a portable tripod . . .' (*Works and Days* 651–9).

It was some later writer who whimsically imagined a head-to-head competition between Hesiod and his near-contemporary Homer, taking place at Chalcis in Euboea. According to this fantasy, the two bards, generally saluted as the founding fathers of Classical literature, trade line for line snatches of poetic wit and folksy wisdom. Hesiod takes the prize. But the content and outcome of this occasion are not so significant as its imaginary purpose. Between them, Hesiod and Homer established and exemplified the principle of positive strife. Contests, challenges, disputes, and abrasion were the necessary trials of all creative endeavour. No economic success came from a life of ease. No great art was born without fierce rivalry.

In another of his works, Hesiod listed the several offspring of *Eris* (*Theogony* 226), including 'Death' and 'Destruction', but above all 'Toil' (*Ponos*), which becomes, as we shall see, a key word in the Greek athletic vocabulary. Homer, for his part, would be glorified as the poet who extracted his song from war; himself the 'glorifier' of men who proved heroes on the battlefield.

Unlike Hesiod, Homer did not distinguish two types of strife in the abstract. Instead, he kept his audience intermittently aware that the conflict which brought renown to heroes was also laden with grief. So it is without irony when Achilles – whom no warrior at Troy can match in his capacity for multiple homicide – sighs to his mother: '*Would that strife might disappear from among men and gods!*' (*Iliad* 18.107). And it is with a palpable sense of relief that Homer signals the end of his epic about 'the wrath of Achilles' with a detailed account not of some climactic killing spree, but of heroes doing battle without their swords and spears.

War minus the shooting finally transpires in the penultimate book of the *Iliad*. Homer's narrative has taken us through the momentous death of Patroklos, Achilles' dearest friend, at the hands of Hector, the Trojan champion; the determined and reckless dispatch of Hector in retaliation from Achilles; the spiteful dragging and defilement of Hector's body by Achilles; and the grim cremation of Patroklos, which includes the execution of twelve Trojan prisoners, again for sheer vengeance, by Achilles. At last, as if surfeited with bloodshed and bereavement, Achilles mellows in his mood. More precisely, he assumes a philanthropic role which later Greeks would dignify with the title *agônothetês*, meaning the sponsor, president, and chief umpire of an *agôn*, or 'contest'.

As soon as we realize that this Greek concept of *agôn* leads to our word 'agony', we are warned that 'games' is too frivolous as a translation for *agônes* wherever they occur in a Classical context. For the time being, however, we may classify what happens in Book 23 of Homer's *Iliad* (lines 262–897) as 'funeral games'. The pyre of Patroklos is still smouldering when Achilles bids everyone sit down while he gathers prizes (*aethla*: the same word, also spelled as *athla*, can entail both 'contests' and 'prizes') for the trials to come. Capacious cauldrons, handled tripods – such as Hesiod won – and assorted quadrupeds are on offer; also several pretty girls who can sew, and some useful lumps of pig-iron.

Ostensibly the sequence of contests which Achilles oversees is secular – at least, not preceded by any invocation to the gods. And Homer does not care to tell us why his heroes thought it fit to conclude a cremation with such 'games'. The contests simply come as part of the funerary rites of a highly honoured individual, and are described with the credible zest of an enthusiast. Homer was not a war reporter, still less a sports commentator. But if the world he versifies is a blend of historical romance and 'realities' of the eighth century BC, we can suppose that the scale and pitch of the contests (heroic) and their occasion (the funeral of mighty Patroklos) are the stuff of fantasy; while their details are drawn from contemporary practice.

There is no formal venue for the eight different contests featured in Homer's narrative. An Athenian vase-painter of the sixth century BC has left us a fragment of his vision of Homeric spectators cheering from

2. Chariots and crowds at the 'games of Patroklos': fragment of an Athenian black-figure bowl painted by Sophilos *c.*570 BC. The legend *PATROKLUS: ATLA* is spelled out in retrograde, as normal for the period; with Achilles identified among the spectators.

a grandstand (Fig. 2). This is an anachronism, for the stadia as such were not distinct structures back in Homer's time. So the first event, chariot-racing, does not take place in a hippodrome but in open tracts of the Trojan plain, with starting order determined by a drawing of lots, and a distant 'look-out' (*skopos*) posted at the designated turning-point. From the generosity of its assigned prizes, and its claim on Homer's poetic attention, we see that this event was the most important of the eight contests, with senior warriors such as Diomedes and Menelaus eager to take up the reins. But Homer loses no time in making us aware that his Greek heroes were not joining the competition just for fun. Each man wants nothing but to win – whatever it takes.

Great bravery is required in driving a chariot at high speed, and much skill too. It is Nestor, the most venerable of all the Greeks at Troy, who makes this explicit in his pre-race counsel to one of the participants. To win prizes demands, above all, 'cunning intelligence' (*mêtis*: lines 313–14).

The will to win, plus the resort to winning by guile, are potentially explosive. And indeed Homer's charioteers erupt into murderous anger, as fouls and injuries multiply. Achilles then proves the perfect arbiter. With his mollifying words – and his genial readiness to fetch out more prizes – quarrels subside into gracious gestures of mutual respect. So Achilles drafts the moral prelude for his own enormous concession (which will come in line 891) – that Agamemnon's power is supreme. Homer's epic had commenced with the bitter rift between Achilles and Agamemnon, overall commander of the Greek forces at Troy. Arising from what might seem a relatively trivial matter, this dispute had swollen so great with intransigence and pride that reconciliation seemed impossible . . .

Before that moment comes, though, there is more action to relate, and it is far from gentle. 'Hurtful boxing' comes next: a slogging, bone-splintering affair, with the volunteer contenders wrapping their knuckles in ox-hide thongs. Still, while the winner prevails with a crashing knock-out blow, he does assist his victim into the upright position – to be dragged off semi-conscious and sputtering blood. Wrestling follows, between Odysseus and Ajax, where again intelligence counts as much as sheer strength; and once more Achilles shows his eirenic spirit, declaring both men joint winners. Then, with brisk acceleration of his own poetic pace, Homer takes us through the running-race, the mock armed combat, the hurling of a weight, the archery, and finally the javelin-throw.

The war at Troy is not over; yet the wrath of Achilles is spent. And while Homer does not pause to moralize on the therapeutic benefits of these athletic exertions, it is implicit that heroes are happiest when at play like this. So when Vergil – Homer's counterpart in the writing of epic for Rome, in the early first century AD – came to imagine an afterlife for the heroes of Troy, he put them in a lush and ample land of their own: the Elysian Fields, a netherworld where retired warriors could plant their unnecessary spears in the ground, and devote themselves to the joy of fighting. The Trojans' well-earned post-humous pension is described. It consists of feasting and songs – and also the raising of glossy steeds, the polishing of brazen chariots, contending in an arena of grass, throwing each other on soft yellow sand (*Aeneid* 6. 637–59).

The feasts and songs we can understand: but what of the rest? Why must the heroes still wrestle, race, and compete, investing so much gratuitous physical effort – except by some addictive, incorrigible habit? Say that they are 'keeping fit', and then ask: fit for what? Their battles were fought long ago. So Vergil seems here to be indulging or perpetuating a sort of symptomatic trait – a quintessential reflex among epic heroes that defines them as 'heroic'. If that was Vergil's aim, then he was anticipating what would later be diagnosed as a prime explanatory feature of Classical Greek culture: a love of competing wherever competition was possible; a desire 'to be best', so strong that even death could not suppress it.

'The Agonistic Spirit'

Historically, it remains impossible to prove that a head-to-head battle between the two bards Homer and Hesiod ever took place; the closest they ever got to each other was probably as 'twinned' honorific statues, as at Olympia (Pausanias 5.26.2). *Spiritually*, though, it is plausible: in the sense that many of the classic texts of Greek literature can be accurately described as 'competition entries'. The works of Aeschylus, Sophocles, Euripides, Aristophanes – these were all written in the hope of carrying off a prize at occasions we usually refer to as dramatic 'festivals', but which the Greeks knew better as 'contests', *agônes*. Many of the prize-winning works by playwrights of Classical Athens have been lost; but some enjoy the remarkable tribute of being successfully performed on stage over 2,500 years after their original production.

We are less directly informed about the quality of equivalent *mousikoi agônes* that brought forth virtuoso performances on the flute or the lyre, and we must speculate about the sounds made by choruses singing 'dithyrambs' in honour of the god Dionysos, also a regular medium of intensely prestigious rivalry in Athens and other Greek city-states. But the circumstantial evidence is there all the same. Whether presenting a case in court, or throwing clay upon the potter's wheel, the opportunity of turning any activity into a contest was pursued. (Classical Greek often refers to a lawsuit as an *agôn* – similar to our 'trial'; for an example of awarding honours to ceramic skill at Athens in the fourth century BC, see *IG* II–III.3.6320.)

A fetish for competing; a pervasive, abrasive eagerness for outdoing the opposition in any field of human endeavour: is this what ultimately explains 'the glory that was Greece' – the cultural bundle of literature, science, philosophy, mathematics, art, and architecture which even by Vergil's time was acknowledged as something special? One influential nineteenth-century writer who thought so was Friedrich Nietzsche (1844–1900). Nietzsche made his name as a Classical philologist in the early 1870s with a pedantic analysis of the text purporting to record the challenge between Homer and Hesiod. Today he is better known for his more extravagant declarations about the need for certain humans to tri-umph shamelessly over others – declarations that were later extracted from context and put to the intellectual service of a German Third Reich. As we shall see, the National Socialists in twentieth-century Germany claimed particular affinity with the athletic-militaristic ideals of ancient Greece; so Nietzsche's 'superman' (*Übermensch*) may readily be envisaged as the lantern-jawed Neo-Classical hulk who looms up in Nazi imagery. But Nietzsche's characterization of Classical culture dominated by 'the agonistic spirit' (*der agonale Geist*) was not revolutionary. He was only relaying – in his own vigorous style – a doctrine already entrenched in the thinking of the pioneer 'cultural historian' Jacob Burckhardt; and both Nietzsche and Burckhardt were indebted to the philosophy of history outlined in the 1820s by G. W. F. Hegel (1770–1831).

It was Hegel who advanced the theory that epochs or periods of history could be explained by reference to prevailing 'Spirits' (*Geisten*). Whether this took the form of a 'Spirit of the People' (*Volksgeist*) or a 'Spirit of the Age' (*Zeitgeist*) does not matter for our purposes; and we can overlook Jacob Burckhardt's denial that he was a doctrinaire 'Hegelian'. The broad truth is that Hegel laid out the intellectual groundwork for *Geistesgeschichte*, the sort of 'cultural history' that would encompass people, places, and decades within a defined 'world-view' (*Weltanschauung*).

Jacob Burckhardt's greatest enterprise was to create,

in 1860, such a history for post-medieval Italy – making connections between art, religion, literature, science, and scholarship that gave fresh and persuasive coherence to the concept of an 'Italian Renaissance'. His effort to do something similar for ancient Greece is not so well known today, but it was a popular lecture course at Basel University in the 1870s, and that was probably where Burckhardt's younger colleague and admirer Nietzsche heard how an entire stretch of Greek history could be explained by reference to the *agôn*, or contest. Burckhardt took his lead from the copious ancient literary evidence relating to athletics generally, and the Olympic Games in particular. He was quick to see, though, how athletic competition provided a 'mentality' for philosophical dialogues, dramatic performances, political careerism, and scientific inquiry. For Burckhardt, this had to be *the* all-explanatory world-view of the Classical Greeks. Was there anything left untouched by their gleeful notions of effort, struggle, and victory?

The tidiness of Burckhardt's approach is not to be despised. Many of us might feel grateful to the historian who, having made a lengthy reconnaissance of some vast and sprawling terrain, offers us the neat essential summary of what we should look out for as the key features of a certain 'epoch'. But, of course, there are problems with such historical hygiene. Burckhardt defines Greek culture by reference to the *agôn*, but his system begins to collapse as soon as its artificial parameters of time and space are exposed. If 'the agonistic spirit' were so special to the Greeks, then why should we find the literature of early Christian evangelism and martyrdom permeated with 'agonistic' language? Or how was it that the athletic festival of the Greeks at Olympia not only survived but flourished in the Roman Empire?

Hesiod was a canonical author in antiquity: a 'set text' for schoolchildren, a poet whose lines were widely known and often quoted. In so far as Hesiod placed 'Strife' as a guiding principle of existence, a central component of cosmic order, we may claim that 'the Greeks' at large were, as Burckhardt saw, obsessed by or at least disposed towards a culture of contest. But it is important to admit that no Greek writer ever generalized in this way. If an 'agonistic spirit' existed in Classical Greece, it did not come about as an abstract ideal. Even in their most theoretical discussions of how to structure young people's education, Greek philosophers attached practical benefits, for both individuals and society, to the effort of trying to be best in a given activity. In Greek terminology, the dual passions of *philoneikia* ('love of competing') and *philonikia* ('love of winning') are made lexically close to the point of conflation (note that Homer did not define Helen – the abducted princess for whom the Greeks went to war with Troy – as the 'the face that launched a thousand ships' but more prosaically as the 'competition's cause': *Iliad* 22.116). Yet victory was not entirely the end purpose of contest; and contest was not an end in itself. Competing was deemed socially useful. 'The agonistic spirit' of the Greeks ultimately had an institutional basis in Greek society.

The very use of the term 'Greek society' risks over-simplifying. But even cities so ideologically diverse as ancient Athens and Sparta had something in common that was fundamental to their collective organization: the understanding that the security and safe-keeping of a city devolved to its own citizen-body.

Athletics and the Mimicry of Violence

In the second century AD a versatile Greek writer and orator called Lucian, who himself came from Samosata, a city on the Euphrates, far away from Greece, tried to imagine what it would be like if a stranger had visited Athens hundreds of years ago, and witnessed how Athenian citizens were spending their days. Lucian places this imaginary visit around the early sixth century BC, at the time when a foundational civic constitution of Athens was being set in place by the city's legendarily wise chief magistrate, Solon. The visitor hails from southern Russia, the land that the Greeks knew as Scythia. His name is Anacharsis, and he belongs to a people usually classified in Greek terms as 'barbarians'. Barbarian he may be, but his first impression of the Athenians is that *they* are utterly mad.

> Some of them, locked in each other's arms, are tripping one another up, while others are choking and twisting each other and grovelling together in the mud, wallowing like swine ... Others, standing

upright, their bodies covered with dust, are attacking each other with blows and kicks . . . one looks as if he were going to spew out his teeth, unlucky man, his mouth is so full of blood and sand . . . Nobody can easily convince me that men who do these things are not out of their minds.

(From Lucian's *Anacharsis* 1–5; adapted from the translation by A. M. Harmon)

Anacharsis is a spectator at an Athenian gymnasium, the Lyceum. What he sees there strikes him as a sort of mania. The sweat, the oil, the blood, the bestial writhing about in a pit of dust – what on earth is it all about?

The answer, in Lucian's fantasy, is supplied by none other than Solon himself. Eloquently, patiently, and unapologetically, Solon justifies this apparently insane behaviour. To begin with, he draws upon the horti-cultural simile of 'hardening out'. Infants and children may be kept tenderly, like seedlings; if they are to grow to maturity, though, they must be exposed to the rough hazards of life in the open. Then Solon proceeds to a more lofty civic pretext for gymnastic sparring. The city, he says, may have ramparts and walls: but these are only externals. The city indulges these athletes because they are the city's true prophylactics, its main line of defence.

And this is not just a matter of staying supple in case of call-up, or even becoming inured to fear. For Solon, the 'freedom' of the citizens directly depends upon those apparently ridiculous exercises being practised in the gymnasium. Do we see one wrestler flailing to grab hold of a muddied opponent? How else should he practise the dexterity required to rescue a stricken comrade in the thick of the fray?

The amplification of this argument is easy enough. Sprinting on soft sand creates stamina for running on hard ground; discus-throwing puts shield-bearing muscle on the shoulders; exercising naked in the midday sun builds endurance; and so on. The physiological principles here are mostly plausible; and beyond utility in war, there is an aspect of peaceful coexistence that Solon does not neglect to mention. Assuming a distinct tone of superiority over his foreign guest, Solon points out that for all the violence contained in the gymnasium, it is a legal offence for Athenian citizens to carry knives in public. So Athens is not like any fear-ridden barbarian habitat. This is a community based on trust; this is civilization.

Lucian's dialogue between Solon and the bemused Scythian may be a rhetorical exercise – but it is nonetheless consonant with numerous surviving opinions from other (and earlier) Greek sources. Solon's central reason for struggle in the gymnasium does not stray from principles laid down by the most influential philosophers of Classical Greece – Socrates, Plato, and Aristotle. Ultimately, there was only one intent and aim of athletic contests: to feint the stress of battle; to stay sharp and ready for war.

Most of the literary evidence for this reasoning comes from Athens. A sample is sufficient: what that sample reveals may be taken to apply more or less to many other Greek city-states during the fifth and fourth centuries BC (definitely more in the singularly militaristic case of Sparta – so singular that we shall leave it to one side). This is the period when democracy, 'rule by the people', was formally constituted at Athens and elsewhere, with much debate about how citizens should manage civic affairs; also the period when Socrates and his followers articulated the value of leading 'the examined life' – which meant what it implies: the need to rationalize one's behaviour. (Nothing should be 'mindless', least of all violence.)

A fourth-century text, ascribed to Aristotle, leads us straight to the institutional basis we seek. From this historical description of the Athenian *politeia*, we learn that full citizenship – the right to vote – was granted only to men (*The Athenian Constitution* 42). The sons of existing citizens were registered on the city's roll-call when they reached the age of eighteen. This 'coming of age' was known as *ephebeia*, but to understand the term 'ephebe' as 'young man' is not quite accurate: 'cadet' may be better, or anything that conveys the immediate obligation on these lads to enter military training. For one year they would occupy barracks near the city, grouped by the voting-districts to which they belonged. There they would be drilled for physical fitness and weapon-handling skills. One of their official trainers was named as a *paidotribês*, implying that he ensured the ephebes were massaged with oil: though the training was called

hoplomachia, 'fighting with weapons', and included archery and siegecraft, there is little doubt it consisted
mainly of hand-to-hand mock combat, of the sort that
could be practised in the gymnasium. The end of the
course was marked by a public display of proficiency in
the theatre, where each ephebe was awarded a spear and
shield, at state expense. Then came two years of active
duty on patrols in the city's wider territory, on the bor-
ders of Attica.

This is a straightforward account of a straightforward
process: defining military service as a prime condition of
citizenship. Specialists in the history of warfare might
also want to add some comment on the peculiar importance of rigorous physical seasoning in this context. The
spear and shield given to the ephebes (to which they
swore an oath of honour: Pollux 8.10.5) were two key
items of equipment necessary for the etiquette of fighting
developed by the Greek city-states, a military mode characteristic of the Greek *polis* since its early formation in
the eighth century BC. One soldier carrying a shield and
spear was known as a 'hoplite'; but the salient feature of
'hoplite warfare' was its dependence upon a tightly coherent unit of soldiers operating together. Assembled by
ranks *en bloc*, the hoplites used shields large enough to
overlap each other, forming a 'phalanx'. They wore
greaves to protect their lower legs, and sometimes also a
corselet; after the shield, however, the most important
piece of their protective panoply was a bronze helmet,
designed to cover as much of the head as possible.

Why do we need to know this? Because, while conceding that soldiers down the ages generally find the experience of combat exhausting and terrible, military historians have identified the hoplite system as particularly demanding of physical and psychological resilience. When two Greek city-states agreed to meet in battle, a suitable open plain was fixed as the venue. Once the commitment to engage was made, there were to be no preliminary skirmishes, no ambushes, no raids or flanking attacks. The encounter should be head-on and decisive: a one-off showdown. Two phalanxes faced each other, and at a signal they advanced towards a direct clash. Those hoplites in the front ranks were most likely to die, and therefore most susceptible to panic; but a phalanx breaking up was tantamount to defeat. If just a few men lost their nerve, the entire unit could fall apart.

For those in search of it, there is scattered evidence in Greek literature alleging not only panic in the hoplite phalanx but also nausea, paralysis, incontinence, and the sheer resort to self-preservation. Equally, there are many testimonials relating to great displays of courage in that situation. Inscribed gravestones, for example, tell proudly of young men who died as 'fighters in the foremost line', *promachoi*. Among such memorabilia we can count the eye-witness stories told about the Athenian philosopher Socrates in battle.

Most citizens of Athens in the fifth century BC had direct experience of hoplite warfare. Socrates was an

Athenian citizen throughout the second half of that century, so it is no surprise that he had a military record. By all accounts he gave distinguished service, without self-seeking histrionics (one reason for keeping fit, he said, was to be able to flee from trouble on the battlefield: Xenophon, *Memorabilia* 3.12.4). The most emotive citation of what would today be termed 'disregard for personal safety' on the part of Socrates comes, admittedly, from a highly partisan source – Alcibiades, as reported in Plato's *Symposium* (220d–221b: for more on the rapport between Socrates and Alcibiades, see p. 49). But other sources corroborate the image of a staunch comrade in the phalanx; and from the Socratic opinions transmitted as if verbatim by his closest successor, Plato, we sense the authentic voice of experience whenever the topic of courage arises.

The ancient Greek word for 'courage' is *andreia*, which translates literally as 'manliness'. But it is an important tenet of Socrates' teaching that courage can be inculcated – in men *and* women. In one of Plato's earliest dialogues (philosophical inquiries presented as conversations between Socrates and his associates) it is Laches, a former comrade-in-arms of Socrates, who draws upon personal reminiscence of Socrates' own valour (*Laches* 180d) to launch a discussion of the meaning of courage. The debate itself is not conclusive – Socrates was intellectually allergic to conclusions – yet there is no question that the quality of fortitude can be put into the educational curriculum. Courage can be acquired by study; with practice, the soul becomes permeated with the necessary skill for dealing with duress, risks, and the danger of death.

Socrates did most of his teaching around the precincts of Athenian gymnasia and wrestling-schools; it was hardly necessary for him to explain further. For a more prescriptive deliberation, we must turn to the mature Plato's *Laws*, where principles of ideal government are explored in practical detail. Plato considered athletic exercise, along with music, a core element in the raising of virtuous citizens. In various sections of the *Laws* (795d; 814, 830c–d, 833a–b) he addresses the rapport between athletics and the 'complicity of war'.

Plato's advice here is very precise. So 'upright wrestling' (*orthôs palê*) is useful for war – but not wrestling on the ground. 'Shadow-skirmishing' (*skiamachein*) to learn rapid hand-reflexes (*cheironomein*) is approved; so too the staging of sham-fights using blunt-tipped spears, soft missiles, and suchlike. Once a month, exercises should be carried out wearing full battle-gear. Most indicative of Plato's approach, perhaps, is the approval he gives to a special sort of armed dance long practised at Athens, the *Pyrrhichê*. Performed by men carrying their hoplite shields and spears, to some kind of quicktime musical accompaniment, the *Pyrrhichê* was evidently a spectacular and highly energetic routine.

It represents modes of eluding all kinds of blows and shots by swervings and duckings and side-leaps

upward or crouching . . . and also . . . active postures
of offence. *Laws* 815a

We have arrived at a Platonic essence of athletics in
ancient Greece. This armed dance is patently an act of
mimicry. It approximates as closely as possible to the
tumult of battle stations; it is the most vivid evocation of
the stress of a hoplite clash as might be conjured without
causing serious injury. In other circumstances, such illusion or 'imitation' (*mimêsis*) would be deplored by Plato
as 'untruthful'. Here it is the excellent device of fundamentally civilized human beings: it is war minus the
shooting.

And as if acknowledging the specific place of
Olympia in this militaristic justification of athletics,
Plato suggests a regular civic award for displays of valour
on the battlefield. It is to be a simple olive wreath –
already very well known as the mark of Olympic victory
(*Laws* 943c).

Reprise: Alexander at Miletus

In 494 BC Miletus, one of the leading Greek cities on
the coast of Asia Minor, was surrounded and sacked by a
Persian army. Over a century later, Alexander the Great,
leading his forces onward to the conquest of the Persian
Empire, passed through the city as its 'liberator'. On
display around Miletus he saw many statues of local athletes who had been victorious at the games of Olympia

and Delphi. Alexander exclaimed: 'Where were men with such bodies [*sômata*] when the barbarians laid siege to your city?' (Plutarch, *Moralia* 180).

The comment may have been sarcastic. Here was an array of sleekly muscular prize-winning athletes, put on pedestals in naked splendour as exemplary heroes of the city. But were these demigods of any use in a war situation? Even before Socrates and Plato had rationalized the purpose of athletic endeavour as military training, dissent was being aired about the application of athletics to war.

> I take no account of a man for his prowess at running or wrestling . . . No man is good in war unless he can take the sight of bodily slaughter and is able, at close quarters, to lunge at the enemy. This is excellence, this is the supreme prize for mortals, and the best a young man can aspire to win. It brings benefit to the state and all citizens, when a man does not fail to hold his ground while fighting in the foremost ranks – heedless of the harsh combat, risking his life, displaying a steady spirit and muttering encouragement meanwhile to the man at his side . . .

Such was the definition of a 'good man' (*anêr agathos*) in the words of Tyrtaios, a poet writing for a Spartan audience in the mid-seventh century BC (Fragment 12).

Later, in fifth-century BC Athens, the dramatist Euripides gave voice to a similar grudge against enthusiasts of the gymnasium.

These athletes cannot survive neediness; they're so entrenched in their useless routines, they can hardly adapt when troubles arise. They parade around when in their prime, laden with glory, heroes of the state. But see what happens to them when bitter old age descends: they fade away and fall apart like worn-out clothes. I deplore the Greek custom of lionizing these types – gathering all citizens and voting for the wasteful celebration of victory feasts. For what civic reward is there in one man who comes home with a crown for slippery wrestling? Or in someone with nimble feet, or who can lob a discus, or deal out a neat right hook? Will they go into battle waving a discus, or break through a barrage of shields and scatter an enemy with their fists alone? What fool thinks of sport, when plunged into the thick of battle?

Unlike Tyrtaios, however, this anti-athletic spokesman is not so concerned to focus upon the practicalities of actual combat. The diatribe continues:

Better, I say, to award laurels to those who have proved their stamina in goodness and intellect; to great politicians, the upright and exemplary; to those who steer us out of fights and rivalries by virtue of their eloquence. For those are the ways in which a city becomes great, and by which all Greeks benefit.

(Fragment from the *Autolycus* by Euripides, c.430 BC)

Tyrtaios the Spartan bard may be regarded as eccentric; certainly there is no evidence that the Spartan tradition of rigorous gymnastic upbringing was modified as a result of his outburst. As for the latter passage in Euripides, which is often cited as a stock critique of athletics in ancient Greece, it should be put in perspective. It comes in a farce, or 'satyr-play', for one thing. And if Euripides intended it as a serious complaint, we may wonder whether the playwright was aware of his own susceptibility to 'hawkish' reproach. As a Spartan visitor once pointed out, what Athenians were spending annually on five days of theatrical entertainment in honour of the god Dionysos – some 100,000 drachmas – was money that would go a long way to supporting effective fleets and armies in the field (Plutarch, *Moralia* 348f–349a).

In the Classical literature of military command, a number of distinguished generals are heard to echo or rephrase the implicit critique voiced by Alexander at Miletus – that good athletes do not necessarily make good soldiers. The sentiment is especially savoured in Latin sources, laced with Roman disdain for supposed Greek 'effeminacy'. Typically Julius Caesar, addressing his troops before battle in the course of civil war with arch-rival Pompey, allows himself the gibe that Pompey's army has in its ranks Greeks 'recruited from the gymnasia – spiritless students of wrestling, scarcely able to carry their weapons' (Lucan, *Pharsalia* 7. 270–2).

Two observations need to be made here. The first is that with the rise of large professional armies, as developed by Alexander and his father Philip II of

Macedon during the fourth century BC, naturally the rationale of keeping citizens fit for military service became weakened. Second, and more importantly, the linking of athletics and war as reasoned by the Athenian philosophers was never intended as some necessary or binding equation. The Greek *palaistra*, or wrestling-school, was not supposed to be a factory of human killing-machines. There were no gladiatorial shows in Classical Greece, nor even any mock-combat event in the programme at Olympia. Fundamentally athletics served to commute, channel, and contain violence. In this respect, Greek athletics may be claimed to share the ultimately cathartic or 'purging' purpose of Greek tragic drama.

Once again we can turn to Socrates. The philosopher so full of questions appears, for our purposes, to have all the answers. Socrates could even vouch for the military usefulness of plays and Dionysiac dithyrambs. 'Those who honour the gods best with choruses,' he is reported as saying, 'are the best in war' (Athenaeus, *Deipnosophistae* 628e). How so? This, surely, is psychological insight; a recognition of how much hoplite fighting relied upon collective self-confidence, group morale, and faith in divine support.

Equally Socrates might have cited the legend about the appearance in battle of Classical antiquity's most celebrated athlete, Milo (or Milon) of Croton. Milo will make repeated appearances in this book: he is an irrepressibly looming figure in the history and romance of ancient sport. Though it is apocryphal, one of the many stories attached to his name may be enough to summarize our argument here.

During the late sixth century BC, the citizens of the Greek colony of Croton in South Italy were obliged to muster an army against Sybaris, another Greek colony nearby. The encounter was to settle a dispute between the two cities; and the Sybarites expected to win, fielding a phalanx that outnumbered the men of Croton by no less than three to one.

The Sybarites counted without Milo, six times victor in the wrestling at Olympia. Milo went at the head of Croton's forces, in the front line. Milo was famed as a phenomenal strongman, physically gigantic. But the tale of his rout of the enemy does not so much turn on Milo's show of strength as his extraordinary, talismanic battle-dress. He sallied forth wearing all of his Olympic victory-wreaths – and the garb of every wrestler's divine hero, Herakles. How the accoutrements of a lion's pelt and a knotty club fitted with hoplite gear we are not told. The very sight of Milo apparently caused panic in the Sybarite ranks, and delivered a miraculous victory to Croton (Diodorus Siculus 12.9). And for all we know, the contest ended there and then, without blood shed by anyone: war minus the shooting.

2

IN TRAINING FOR
BEAUTIFUL GOODNESS

Going to the gym is not a strange concept to most modern people. (It might be a rare *practice*.) We know what it means. Going to the gym is about looking good, feeling good, living longer. For some it may be prompted by doctor's orders; for others, the gym is a place to socialize, or a venue charged with erotic potential. Though we have not yet coined a verb quite equivalent to the ancient Greek *gymnazesthai*, 'to gymnify', and we remain timid about the etymological implication of that verb – to be naked – this is one institution of Classical antiquity that has made a powerful comeback in the modern world.

The return of the gymnasium and the reinvention of 'the Olympic Games' are intertwined historical phenomena: both can be traced to the second half of the nineteenth century and the discovery of leisure as a commodity within industrial societies. The nexus of institutional gymnasium and formal athletic festivals was also prevalent in the Classical world. For over a thousand years, the athletic contests at ancient Olympia attracted competitors and spectators from all around the Mediterranean and beyond. The continuity, the primacy, and the collective enthusiasm of that tradition cannot be understood without first excavating the central importance of the gymnasium in the urban communities of the Classical Mediterranean. (This is not to say that rural peasants were excluded from the Games: see p. 201.)

There are aspects of Greek and Roman gymnasium conduct to which we may easily relate – as born-again believers in physical culture. But perhaps we should begin with an unfamiliar notion. What if gymnasium attendance was deemed one of the normal obligations of citizenship – like paying tax?

Going to the Gym: a Civic Duty

To say that the city-states of Classical Greece expected everyone within their walls to maintain rigorous levels of physical fitness is an over-simplification. But it is not unrealistic to imagine that many of the 'big names' who come to mind from Classical Greek history and culture probably spent some time each day exercising in the precincts of a gymnasium. Sophocles was a successful writer, Perikles a busy politician, and Socrates a committed philosopher – but it is unlikely that any of them neglected his regular workout. If ancient reports are credible, Socrates' most devoted pupil, Plato, even gained honours in wrestling at one of the major Panhellenic meetings (most likely the Isthmian Games: Servius, *ad Aen.* 6.668).

In Plato's ideal state, the civic values of daily gymnastic discipline are clearly defined (*Republic* 403–12). Plato distrusts over-specialization of diet and training routines, because it renders athletes unadaptable and sluggish, needing too much sleep. Citizens of the perfect polity should attend the gymnasium to keep themselves generally alert, free from ill-health, and ready for eventual war or hardship. A fine body does not guarantee a fine mind: but decent-thinking people will strive to keep their bodies trim and avoid excess of food and drink. Hard physical exercise is coupled with inspiring music as complementary factors in Plato's definition of a well-balanced, finely-tuned, and 'philosophical' education.

Plato is not here extolling a democratic ideal of physical fitness; rather, instructing a leisured elite on how to make best use of their time. All the same, it is clear that the success of regular athletic meetings at Athens, Olympia, and elsewhere partly depended upon – and in turn, nurtured – the *political* expectation, widespread around the Greek world, that good citizens kept themselves, or aspired to be, in 'good shape' (*eumorphia*). To appreciate the pervasive force of that expectation, we may find a philosopher's theories less telling than evidence laid straight out on the ground.

Gymnasia *in situ*

It is time to introduce Pausanias, an author to whom frequent reference will be made throughout this book. Born on the coast of Asia Minor in the early second century AD, Pausanias was a traveller through Greek lands that had for several centuries belonged to the Roman Empire. He had a strong sensibility towards what might be called the 'Greek heritage' wherever it survived. He also had a very clear idea of what, in the course of his journeyings, qualified as a city or *polis*. Explicitly, he tells us that a habitation that lacked a gymnasium was not a city (*Guide to Greece* 10.4.1: all future references are to the same work).

So the gymnasium is one of the key formal criteria of city status, taking its place along with the market-square (*agora*) and council-house (*bouleuterion*). It was a recognizable urban feature. A century before Pausanias, clear guidelines had been established for what a gymnasium should look like in terms of its architectural structure (Vitruvius, *On Architecture* 5.11). There was also a general understanding of what the word 'gymnasium' meant: etymologically it is tied to the Greek word *gymnos*, 'unclad', and so entailed a place where one went to exercise without clothes on: 'nuditorium' is how it literally translates. But this clarity of purpose is misleading. The gymnasium as a social institution in antiquity was often much more – and sometimes rather less – than a place where one simply went to strip off and exercise. And while it was indeed a defining aspect of the Greek *polis* or Roman *urbs*, the gymnasium also served as a sort of retreat from civic life; an antidote, as it were, to some of those other key components of the Greek or Roman city, in particular the main space for daily business – the *agora* or *forum*.

Gymnasia as formal enclosures do not seem to have existed in the age of Homer (eighth century BC) or earlier. In fact there is so far no surviving material evidence for any Greek gymnasium in existence prior to the mid-fourth century BC, though we presume (from circumstantial evidence) that dedicated sites and buildings were in use by the middle of the sixth century. Of the three famous prototypes located around Athens, one – the Lyceum – was reportedly monumentalized by the sixth-century tyrant of Athens, Peisistratos; with another, the Academy, owing its boundary walls to an expensive project by his son Hipparchus. But along with a third, the Cynosarges, all these Athenian gymnasia were thought to have been in rudimentary existence by the time of the archaic lawgiver Solon (*c.*600 BC).

Though their remains are elusive, we know that each of these early Athenian gymnasia was situated close to running water – the Lyceum by the banks of the River Kephisos, the Academy and the Cynosarges by the streams of the Eridanus and Ilissos respectively. Bath complexes (certainly those with heated water) did not become integral to gymnasium design until the Roman period, but a ready source of fresh water was always a priority in locating the Classical gymnasium. Otherwise there was no set rule to determine where gymnasia must be situated. At Nicaea in Bithynia (modern Iznik in Turkey) the gymnasium occupied the very centre of a gridded town layout; while the Academy of Athens lay in suburbs; and the main gymnasium of Sparta, the Platanistas – so called because it was shaded by plane trees (*platanoi*) – was set apart on a river island. No topography, it seems, was so challenging that it defied the construction of a gymnasium: witness the early fourth-century BC example at Delphi, dramatically arranged at altitude in the terraced slopes of Mount Parnassus (**Fig. 3**).

A bird's eye view of the two-tiered gymnasium at Delphi surveys some key sporting facilities. On the upper tier there is an elongated level area (not far short of the average stadium length of about 200 metres) that was once colonnaded and roofed over. The Greek term for this is a *xystos*, which originally meant just a patch of ground cleared and raked over; later, however, it denoted a covered area for sprinting practice in wet or very hot weather, to be contrasted with a parallel track (*paradromos*) that was open to the elements – as we also see clearly at Delphi.

The gymnasium, then, should be somewhere sufficiently spacious for the provision of these one-way running tracks, whose surface was kept soft and firm by regular raking and rolling. Spaces for jumping and throwing were also provided, and efforts made to create

3. View of the gymnasium at Delphi.

shaded avenues where perhaps some gentle strolling was allowed: the Athenian Academy, for instance, was land-scaped thanks to an initiative from Kimon, the rival and predecessor of Perikles, and became celebrated for its welcome cool aroma of woodbine and lime blossom. What else was normally expected? At Delphi, the answer is laid out for view on the lower terrace (**Fig. 4**). Here lie the remains of a large circular plunge bath, some showers and wash-basins, and a *palaistra*, or 'wrestling-school'. This last is recognizable by its characteristic form, a courtyard with cubicles around the square or rectangular shallow recess known as a *skamma*, the sand-pit where hand-to-hand combats were practised.

Most ancient gymnasia included, or were attached to, a *palaistra*. Eventually, it seems, the terms *gymnasion*

4. The plunge bath at Delphi.

5. View of the *palaistra* at Olympia, with plan (opposite).
    Partly restored, the structures belong originally to the third
    century BC.

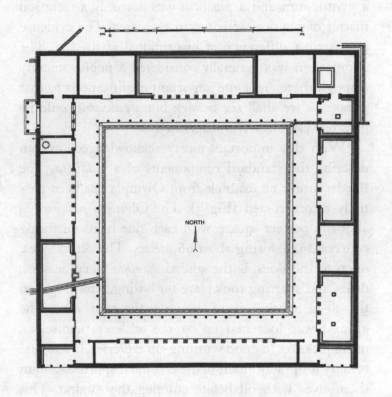

and *palaistra* could be more or less synonymous. We should recognize, however, that discrimination between a gymnasium and a *palaistra* was not only a technical matter of physical activities in each area. The evidence points to a difference of institutional status too. The gymnasium was generally considered a public amenity (though there are some important qualifications to that phrase, as we shall see below); but a *palaistra* could be privately established and operated.

With this important nicety acknowledged, we can describe the standard components of a *palaistra*. The third-century BC example from Olympia has been partially reconstructed (**Fig. 5**). The Olympia *palaistra* is almost a perfect square, with each side of its enclosing courtyard measuring about 66 metres. The central area, open to the skies, is the sanded *skamma* where lessons, drills, and sparring took place for boxing, wrestling, and the all-in fighting event known as the *pankration*. The ground was loosened up by the athletes themselves, using pickaxes (a good warming-up exercise). It was customary for practitioners of these combat sports to anoint themselves with oil before entering the sandpit. This habit of lubrication served cosmetically to keep sun-beaten skin moist. But because it made wrestling holds almost impossible to effect, body powders were also applied. Some sort of mud-wrestling might take place; and one wrestling exercise was simply called *alindesis*, 'rolling in dust', as horses do. At any rate, athletes came away from the *skamma* routinely coated in a mixture of dust, oil, sweat, and probably blood too – so they needed thorough ablutions. Water would be available, but more immediately effective was the resort to scraping, *apoxyesis*. So it came about that a key gadget of the *palaistra* was the curved and channelled blade called a strigil (after the Latin, *strigilus*; *stlengis* in Greek). Its deployment can be seen often enough in scenes on Greek vases, and a statue-type of an athlete running a strigil over his body was much admired for centuries after its original creation (*c.*350–340 BC), being dubbed simply 'The Scraper', or *Apoxyomenos* (**Fig. 6**). The strigil was carried about almost like a symbol of *palaistra* membership, along with an *ayrballos*, or oil-flask; these are often found among the few personal belongings deposited in a Greek grave and as such often assumed by archaeologists to be posthumous badges of masculinity.

A *palaistra* had benches around its courtyard where members could rest and watch others training, and as the design of the Olympia *palaistra* shows, many separate rooms were also gathered within the enclosure. Individually it is hard to say which room served which purpose, but a list can be made of some specific functions we know to have been assigned to these units. Indispensable was the *apodyterion*, the changing room. There should also be a club room, or *ephebeion*, where the 'adolescents' (*epheboi*) could gather and socialize: *palaistrai* were predominantly for active use by junior male citizens, with seniors mostly either instructing or watching. Then there was a range of rooms set aside for

6. Bronze figure of an *Apoxyomenos*, late fourth century BC. Height 1.94 m. Recovered off the Croatian island of Vele Orjule in the Adriatic Sea, this statue was probably taken from a Greek site to decorate an early Imperial Roman villa or gymnasium.

particular stages of self-preparation and training drills. These might include an *elaiothesion*, an 'oiling-room'; a *konisterion*, where dusting powder (*konis*) was stored in baskets; and a space where punch-bags (*korikoi*: sacks or bladders filled with fig seeds and sand) were suspended. At Olympia, a simple large bathtub, 1.40 metres deep, was set into the northeast corner of the courtyard. Along the north side there was a brick-tiled pavement, just under 25 metres in length. It is not clear what purpose this served: some have supposed it was a space for playing quoits or other games.

So much for the basic architecture and overt purpose of the Greek gymnasium and *palaistra*. In fact the heyday of building these institutions came in the 'Hellenistic' age (323–31 BC), after the Greek cities submitted to first Macedonian and subsequently Roman control. But already by the late fifth century BC, it seems that not every gymnasium or *palaistra* was resounding to the shouts and thuds of extreme physical effort. One of Plato's philosophical dialogues, the *Lysis*, describes an encounter between Socrates and some young friends, plausibly taking place in the last decade of the fifth century. In the opening scenario of this encounter, Socrates is making his way from one old gymnasium (the Academy) towards another (the Lyceum), when he stops by a *palaistra* 'of recent construction'. 'And what', asks Socrates ingenuously, 'do you spend your time doing here?' The answer is not 'wrestling', as we might expect, but 'words' – 'mostly words' (*polla en logois*). Socrates is invited to step inside and join the talking-shop. The subject for discussion is the nature of friendship. But why should a school for martial arts be an apt locale for philosophical debate; and in particular, a debate about the loving relationships between men? To answer those questions, we need to sketch some further social history of the Greek gymnasium.

Philosophers and Pederasts

As pictured in the opening of the *Lysis*, it was not bizarre for Socrates to be strolling from one gymnasium to another in search of opportunities to converse, debate, and teach amongst the young men of Athens. However much its daily attendance might be rationalized as keeping dutifully fit for military service, and however strenuous its programme, the Classical Athenian gymnasium was nonetheless a place of ease and recreation. In a society in which child-rearing and all domestic chores were carried out by women or slaves, and most manual labour assigned to low-born artisans or immigrant workers (metics), the males who constituted the voting citizen body – numbering perhaps 50,000 or so around the time of Perikles, in the mid-fifth century – had ample free time at their disposal. For some, of course, political duties were time-consuming; and for all, as we have stressed, the call-up for war was never far away. But once these men had completed their primary learning (normally by the age of fourteen), they were at liberty to pursue 'higher education' as they pleased – so long, of course, as their fathers could afford it. The Greek word for leisure is *scholê*, and its radical associations in English are significant. 'Leisure', *scholê*, becomes identified with 'how leisure is used', and thus with 'studying'. So a 'school' is a place where studying is done, and a 'scholar' someone who studies. In the gymnasia of Athens, Socrates was likely to meet the most receptive audience for his moral vocation of 'thinking aloud': maturing young men, generally eager to prove that they could flex their minds no less vigorously than their muscles.

It is sometimes suggested (by voices ancient and modern) that gymnasia were subverted or surreptitiously infiltrated by philosophers, turning centres of physical excellence into porticoes of pernickety disputation. This is not quite accurate in the case of Classical Athens. When Plato set up his school at Athens *c*.385 BC, it was in a house and garden adjacent to the Academy gymnasium (itself so called because it occupied a site sacred to the memory of an obscure Bronze Age hero called Akademos). True, Plato could hope to attract fee-paying pupils from among the affluent types who frequented the gymnasium; but there is no evidence that he intended to divert them. As outlined above, his system of education ideally aimed for harmony between intellectual and physical exertions.

Only gradually did the proximity of school and gymnasium produce the association we know as 'Plato's

Academy' – which in turn gives us such cognate terms as 'academia' and 'academic'. But when the most distinguished graduate from Plato's school came to set up his own institution, he too chose a gymnasium site. Aristotle's 'Peripatetic' philosophy gained its name from a covered walkway (*peripatos*) that he rented in the grounds of the Lyceum (a place sacred to Apollo's 'wolfish' guise, Apollo Lykeios). Over the centuries, again, the fame of lecture-hall and library came to eclipse the reputation of the gymnasium as a place for exercise; with the Aristotelian Lyceum eventually lending its name, in French, to any secondary school (*lycée*). Less resonance has survived from the other archaic Athenian gymnasium, the Cynosarges. But it too was adopted as a base for a philosophical sect, in this case the Cynics, whose nickname ('the Dogs') may have been enough to endear them to the site (arising from some local legend, 'Cynosarges' translates as 'white dog', or 'fast dog').

Not all of the philosophers pitching their message in or nearby gymnasium precincts showed an equal commitment to calibrating a refined balance between body and soul. But it is fair to say that they shared the core Socratic mission to teach the value of an 'examined life'. Plato maintained that philosophy, rightly conducted, would produce valuable members of the political community. However, he operated in the groves of the Academy because it was topographically, and purposefully, set aside from the daily cares of politics and commerce. For leisure, *scholê*, could also be defined negatively as *apragmosynê*, 'freedom from business'. Those who came to the Academy gymnasium were taking respite from public and business affairs. In this pleasant and fragrant place, undisturbed by pressing demands of the day, they could address what were (for Socrates and Plato, at least) the more important issues of life. How can we be good? What happens when we die? How do we know what we know? Or the question which dominates the *Lysis*, and other Platonic dialogues: what is it that draws us to another person – that makes us fall in love? The latter was a poignantly appropriate topic of inquiry because in Classical Athens, as in other Greek cities, the gymnasium tended to be not only a very sociable place, but also an institution seething with erotic interest and excitement.

A commonsense attitude to this phenomenon might claim it was hardly surprising. Assemble the gilded youth, have them stripped naked and burnished with oil, then put them to rolling around with each other in a sandpit – who could be amazed if certain arousals and affinities ensued? (For our great-grandparents, veiled over with such phrases as 'the unspeakable vice of the Athenians'.) In fact it was a normal practice, in the *palaistra*, for a wrestler to tie a string knot around his foreskin, probably to inhibit the sudden awkwardness of an erect phallus. But there is more to it than physiological response. To say that gymnasia were homosexual 'pick-up joints' is to put it too crudely. But they were undoubtedly arenas for pederasty, the custom whereby men – including men of high office, and happily married men – became, in public, the infatuated lovers of boys.

There is neither space nor need here to rehearse the supposed archaic behavioural functions of pederasty in Greek society: broadly, the practice is usually glossed as some kind of initiation rite. For our purposes, it is sufficient to be aware that *paiderastia*, 'the strong desire for boys', was not in itself a shameful pursuit. On the contrary, in the eyes of Plato and others, it could be the most ennobling and honourable form of love in human experience. But it was hedged around with certain ethical codes and legal boundaries. The gymnasium was a site where both the objects and the rules of pederasty were exposed.

The objects of pederastic enthusiasm were, by definition, the boys: tautly toned teenagers, out of puberty but not yet using a razor; outstanding young athletes, whose naked bodies (as the poets would put it) shimmered with the longing and potential for the victor's crown – and yet who had a becoming modesty about them, appearing almost reckless of their astonishing beauty. The rules of pederasty were of more concern to their fathers. Paternal consent was required for a courtship to proceed. If permission were forthcoming, then by all means the senior lover (*erastês*) might go to the gymnasium to watch and admire his junior loved one (*erômenos*), and possibly present certain conventional tokens of affection: a hoop to play with, or perhaps a live hare or roe deer as a pet. But further sexual advances were usually out of place here.

There is a telling moment in one of Plato's best-known dialogues, the *Symposium*, at the point where one of the disciples of Socrates – Alcibiades, a charismatic figure who will appear elsewhere in this book – is describing a rare inversion of pederastic protocol. Young Alcibiades has developed a crush on the venerable Socrates, and believes Socrates to be in love with him – yet is having problems finding some quiet time to express this devotion. Alcibiades proposes that they go to the *palaistra*. Socrates accepts, and they duly wrestle together there, on several occasions. 'But', as Alcibiades exclaims, 'even when there was no one else around, I got no further with him!' (*Symposium* 217c). The implication is that wrestling was one way of getting close to one's beloved; but nudity and close contact in the gymnasium were not a licence for indiscreet sex.

It is necessary to outline such pederastic etiquette because a number of painted vases from Athens appear to illustrate erotic scenes in a gymnastic setting (**Fig. 7**). These may be fantasies – though not without realistic details if studied closely. We learn, for example, that while sexual gratification in a pederastic rapport was one-sided – the boys are mostly shown passive, strangely bemused – actual penetration was rare, with the *erastai* apparently content to rub themselves in between the top of a boy's thighs (evidence for this so-called 'intercrural intercourse' is not forthcoming, beyond what appears on vases). Athenian pottery was mostly painted with a view

7.   Courtship scene on an Athenian black-figured amphora. The
     central youth holds a victory-garland; one of his admirers
     brings a deer.
     Above: wrestlers.

to its use at drinking parties, or *symposia*, where perhaps the carnal aspects of a pederastic relationship were often explored. Even so, it is worth relating the distinctly high-minded intentions with which one symposium was arranged. This sounds 'Platonic'; in fact it is the overture not to Plato's *Symposium*, but a dialogue of the same title written by the Athenian soldier, statesman, and writer Xenophon, set in the year 422 BC.

Xenophon's *Symposium* opens as follows. A prominent citizen of Athens called Kallias is enamoured of a boy named Autolycus. At the Panathenaic Games, Autolycus has triumphed in his age group at the *pankration* fighting event, which despite its violent nature has apparently left his looks unblemished. As a reward, the wealthy Kallias first takes Autolycus and Autolycus' father to see the horse-racing, then stages a grand symposium, in honour of both of them. To render the occasion even more memorable, Kallias also invites Socrates along to the party. The senior guests arrive and take up the reclining positions typical of a symposium (incidentally we may note that Xenophon explicitly mentions that they had all come fresh from gymnasium sessions themselves, with massages and baths). Then Autolycus makes his entrance. He is only a boy – but his presence, as Xenophon describes it, is like some royal epiphany. All eyes are fixed on Autolycus as he modestly takes a couch next to his father. 'Not one of those present,' comments Xenophon, 'failed to feel his soul somehow shaken' by the boy's supreme beauty, shiningly manifest 'like a light in the dark'. The company was struck speechless. But Xenophon also records the reaction of Kallias as *erastês* of Autolycus. Visibly he was enhanced by the power of his love, dignified by the consummate grace of divine *Eros*.

During the discussion that ensues, Socrates will use the example set by Kallias and Autolycus to support his theory that there is a higher or 'heavenly' love that transcends mere physical attraction and genital excitement. But for all that Socrates may cling philosophically to his doctrine of 'dualism' – maintaining an essential division between 'body' and 'soul' – anecdotally it is evident that he himself recognized when a boy appeared compellingly beautiful. And nowhere in the supposed transcriptions of his discourse does Socrates deny that beauty not only delights the eyes of its beholders, but also feeds their souls.

One adjective is enough to describe Autolycus: he is *kalos*, 'beautiful'. So what does that mean? Close to death, Socrates is famously said to have asserted the abstract and absolute status of beauty: 'by means of beauty all beautiful things become beautiful' (*Phaedo* 100e). His followers may have raised their drinking cups to toast this sentiment. But if they wanted to check what it was that conferred beauty on the form of a boy, they had only to look at the images painted upon those very cups – boys with slim waists, broad shoulders, neatly proud buttocks, and springy thighs. As if the images themselves were not explicit enough, the message was spelled out in words: 'So-and-so/this boy is beautiful (*kalos*)' (see Fig. 28). Thousands upon thousands of such images and inscriptions were produced in ancient Athens, and they leave us in no doubt. Men were not born beautiful. They made themselves that way – in the gymnasium.

The Gymnasium as Microcosm: the Beroia Stele

In 1949 a densely inscribed tablet (*stêlê*) came to light from the ancient Macedonian city of Beroia (modern Veroia, west of Thessaloniki). Originally set up during the mid-second century BC, it spells out the rubric to be followed by whoever is appointed *gymnasiarchos*, or 'gymnasium-magistrate'. With its text running to hundreds of lines, one thing is immediately apparent – that the rotating role of *gymnasiarchos* was an onerous responsibility, invariably demanding some financial generosity from its incumbent: we know from other sources that a gymnasiarch was expected to supply so many cups of oil per man, youth, and boy using the gymnasium – or else find others to provide it. The 'gymnasiarchal law of Beroia' itemizes the many administrative duties involved over a year of office, ranging from disciplinary procedures (enforced by fines or floggings) to the organization of special festivals: when the date came round for a relay-race with torches, for example, the gymnasiarch must see to the nomination of umpires, ensure that regulated torches were made ready, and supervise the precise observation of liturgies to the god Hermes.

Much of the Beroia inscription is of rather technical interest. But its very fussiness of detail is revealing of a general truth: that this gymnasium was a world within itself, a microcosm. Self-regulating, with its own system of revenues, this was a club whose membership was strictly selective. The gymnasiarch may well have been a volunteer, with other political commitments around the city; inside the gymnasium, however, he was more of a sovereign than a superintendent, ruling as if by divine right. Gymnasia normally contained altars to heroes and higher powers, and Hermes was the resident deity at the Beroia gymnasium (at the Lyceum Apollo was wor-shipped; Athena at the Academy, with subsidiary shrines to Zeus, Hermes, and Herakles, and, presumably, the mysterious Akademos; while Herakles was presiding genius of the Cynosarges). This meant that any in-fringement of gymnasium discipline could be counted as sacrilege. It also gave immanent sanction to the exclusive codes of gymnasium usage. So it is that the Beroia tablet specifically outlaws the following categories of person from gymnasium premises: slaves, prostitutes, market traders, drunkards, and the mentally deranged.

The ban on slaves – possibly extending to 'freedmen' who had slave origins – is not, for the period, remark-able. Nor does it seem controversial to deny access to alcoholics and lunatics. By 'prostitutes' are probably intended those young men who abused the customs of pederasty and touted themselves as promiscuous 'little buggers' (*kinaidoi*). But what are we to make of the rejection of shopkeepers – literally, 'market-types' (*agoraioi*)? It can only be snobbery: affirmation that this gymnasium was reserved for those who did not care (or need) to hawk and haggle for a living.

A tradition about the Cynosarges gymnasium at Athens records that it was the sporting habitat of 'illegitimates' (*nothoi*) – citizens of half-foreign extraction. We are told that the early fifth-century Athenian leader Themistokles, himself of such origin, cajoled some of his genteel contemporaries into exercising with him there, so helping to break down the distinction between 'low-born' and 'noble' in Athens (Plutarch, *Themistokles* 1). This helps to sustain the reputation of Themistokles as a staunch democrat, but plenty of evidence can be summoned from subsequent Athenian literature to demonstrate that tensions of social rank continued to pervade the city's gymnasia and sporting programmes – not least from Alcibiades, who allegedly took up chariot-racing because he was disgusted by the number of ill-bred commoners to be found in the wrestling contests.

We shall never be able to reconstruct all the delicate nuances of class consciousness at Beroia or Athens, or anywhere else in Classical antiquity. The inscription, of course, has its own specific location in time and place. But we can see well enough that the gymnasiarchal law of Beroia enforces a basic divide within the male gender.

There are those who attend the gymnasium, and those who do not. The latter – denominated as *apalaistroi*, 'men-without-*palaistra*' – may exert themselves as they will in other activities: heaving barrels, crouching over an anvil, or scurrying around in some hot, industrious workshop. Such 'banausic' labour was directly disdained because of its ill-effects upon the body: for all that it might be hard graft, its often sedentary and enclosed nature tended to 'effeminize' the manly form (see Xenophon, *Oikonomikos* 4.2–3). The gymnasium faithful had their own creed. For them, manly excellence (*aretê*) was intrinsically bound up with physical prowess and presence. The athletic body was the beautiful body. And the beautiful body was the outward form of the good, the virtuous individual.

This is a peculiar moral logic which requires further exploration.

Kalokagathia: an Ideal and its Representation

In the ideal Classical city, the paragon-citizen, whose voting rights originated from his availability for military service, kept himself in conspicuously good shape as a matter of political duty, not personal vanity. Yet the gymnasium ambiance was charged with the atmosphere of sexual selection. Even if the obligation to practise combat sports for imminent call-up faded – especially after the development of professional armies, pioneered by the Macedonians in the fourth century BC – the

Greek word *kanon* gives us our 'canonical', which implies a standard to be respected, a central point of authority. If copies from the output of Polykleitos illustrate his rules (one work, the *Doryphoros*, or 'Spear-Carrier', is usually reckoned as constructed according to the sculptor's *Kanon*), then it is clear enough that 'aesthetically successful' in Polykleitan terms means a body dominated by qualities of tautness, symmetry, and balance. A harmony of parts was what Polykleitos appears to have sought, even if that meant neatening up the natural anatomy of human beings into impossibly geometric lines (**Fig. 8**).

Modern physiologists sometimes divide human body shape into three basic 'somatypes': the ectomorph (thin, attenuated), the endomorph (plump, bulging), and the mesomorph (in between). An Athenian drinking cup of the early fifth century shows us clearly the Classical preference for the mesomorphic: beyond some 'good' athletes diligently practising with their javelins, we see the 'bad' forms of lanky youth and chubby youth bickering between themselves (**Fig. 9**). For young men, the pressure to aspire towards a more or less predictable 'Polykleitan' norm – broad shoulders, contoured thorax, firm waist, powerful thighs – was onerous, and literally cast as a norm by one Classical sculptor after another.

Later on, in Roman gymnasia and baths it was *de rigueur* for statues of the Polykleitan ideal to be raised as models for general emulation. The 'Spear-Carrier' was repeatedly copied as a showpiece for some niche or colonnade (**Fig. 10**). How, though, were such exemplary

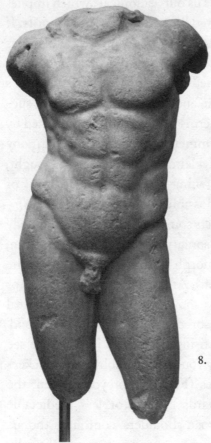

8. Marble torso after the Polykleitan 'Discophorus'. Roman copy, (first century AD), perhaps representing the god Hermes.

bodies to be achieved? The ancient equipment for training scarcely matched the machinery of a modern health club or fitness suite. The concept of progressive resistance was more or less understood (Philostratos, *On Gymnastics* 43), and tenuously illustrated by some of the many stories attached to the hefty personage of Milo of

9. Athletes of various body shapes: exterior of a red-figure Athenian drinking cup (*kylix*) painted by Pheidippos, c.470 BC. The plump boy has boxing-thongs in his hands; his scrawny companion may be attempting a wrestler's lunge, or possibly the starting position of a runner.

10. The Doryphoros: Roman marble copy after a mid-fifth century BC bronze original by Polykleitos. Many Roman copies exist of this type, first identified as the Polykleitan 'Spear-Carrier' in 1863. As copied, however, the figure holds a military lance—not an athletic javelin.

Croton, who legendarily commenced his weight-lifting programme by hoisting a calf onto his shoulders, and continued to do this as the calf grew into a full-sized ox (see, for example, Quintilian, *Institutio Oratoria* 1.9.5; the complementary tale being, of course, that Milo eats the ox). Beyond these myths of prodigious muscular feats (see also Homer, *Iliad* 5.302 and 12.445), archaeology has uncovered two solid attestations of extraordinary human strength in antiquity: from Olympia, the red sandstone boulder weighing 143 kg (315 lbs) with an archaic inscription claiming that a certain Bybon threw it over his head with one hand; and from the island of Thera (Santorini), a volcanic block of 480 kg (over 1,000 lbs) inscribed *c.*500 BC as having been lifted off the ground by some anonymous strongman.

We can assume that muscular development in antiquity derived mainly from stamina-loaded routines of sparring, sprinting, and one-to-one grappling. But regimes of exercise and diet could be followed very rigorously, to judge from one surviving handbook of around the third century AD, the tract *On Gymnastics* attributed to Philostratos. Because Philostratos subscribed to the prevailing Graeco-Roman medical doctrine that human constitutions could be classified according to four basic temperaments or 'humours', depending on the balance of bodily fluids (blood, phlegm, black bile, yellow bile), and a physiognomic system (pioneered by Aristotle) that liked to assimilate body types to animals (leonine, bearlike, and so on), some of his rules will seem quaint. But there are aspects of athletic wisdom in Philostratos that still make very good sense, in particular the structuring of training around a 'four-day cycle' (*tetrad*) of varying intensity. The approach of Philostratos is holistic, and full of practical hints (the value of headbutting a punch-bag, how best to sprinkle dust about one's body, when to sunbathe, and so on).

We also possess some testimonies regarding contests and incentives to motivate gymnasium attendance. A number of gymnasia – notably those in Greek-speaking communities of Hellenistic and Roman Asia Minor – have yielded inscriptions that point to a range of institutional competitions that promoted outstanding bodily beauty, and encouraged related effort. One threefold challenge recurs: the *euexia*, *eutaxia*, and *philoponia*. The *euexia*, implying a good state of 'bodily condition' (*hexis*), was evidently a test of muscular development and posture, with marks awarded for tone, definition, and symmetry. The *eutaxia* ('good order') stressed proficiency at military drills; in the Beroia stele, the *eutaxia* evidently also rewarded blameless behaviour in the gymnasium throughout the year (petty theft and assaults on the gymnasiarch are cited as transgressions). The third category must have recompensed diligent sloggers, being a prize for sheer *philoponia*, 'love of training'.

The physical virtue above all was *euandria*, 'fine manliness'. This was built into the title of a 'manliness contest', the *agôn euandrias*, regularly held at Athens from the late sixth century onwards, under the auspices of the

Panathenaic Games and Xenophon *Symposium* 4.17. Young men would be nominated as representatives of their voting wards or 'tribes', and subjected to various tests of prowess (such as bareback riding) and appearance. The criteria by which a prize-winning body was judged are not known. But we do know the victors received substantial gifts – shields or oxen, for example – and were greeted with multiple garlands, and had ribbons tied around their bodies (**Fig. 11**). Beyond Athens there were other versions of this contest. One held at Elis, near Olympia, was called the *krisis kallous*, 'the judgement of the beautiful'; it was to the glory of the goddess Athena. Another, at Tanagra in Boeotia, was staged by the altar of the god Hermes Kriophoros ('Hermes the Ram-Bearer'): here, the privilege granted to the boy showing most beauty was to carry a ram around the city walls in Hermes' honour. So there was a distinct votive element to these beauty competitions, since excellence of human form was regarded as an insight into divine nature. The sight of a beautiful person could be claimed as something which was pleasing to the eyes of the gods above: this sentiment is repeatedly voiced in the poetry written to celebrate athletic victors (see Chapter 4).

Did the ideal of 'beautiful goodness' entirely revolve around young men? Not quite. Admittedly, beyond the unusual case of Sparta (see p. 118) we cannot say how much, if at all, women frequented gymnasia in the Greek world. But there are some indications from Roman texts

11. Prize-winning boy, as featured on an Athenian red-figure oil-flask (*lekythos*) attributed to the Bowdoin Painter, *c.*480–470 BC. At the base of one of the pillars is a propped-up discus.

12. Female athletes exercising (or possibly performing): detail of
    mosaic pavement from the villa at Piazza Armerina in Sicily,
    fourth century AD.

and images that female exercise sessions were possible –
among these a mosaic in Sicily showing several bikini-
clad girls holding weights in their hands (Fig. 12). As
for the older generation, it is worth noting that the 'fine
manliness' contest set up at Athens included senior
categories, too. The bearded elders who prevailed here
were granted the public triumph of being branch-
carriers in a dedicatory procession to Athena. (The
branches they carried were young shoots of olive, a tree
famous for its green and productive endurance over
many decades.)

'Beauty varies with each age', observed Aristotle

(*Rhetoric* 1361b). In some cities, older men had their own place of exercise (*gerontikê palaistra*). Homer's Nestor offered a literary archetype of the veteran athlete-warrior, accorded great respect despite his tendency to trade at length on glory days of yore. Advanced years were resented in so far as they enfeebled physical prowess; it was always important to maintain a sort of fighting fitness. So Aristotle continues his observation:

> In the young man [*neos*], beauty consists in having a body that can endure all sorts of exertion in running or in violent force [*bia*], and one that is delightful to gaze on. That is why pentathletes are the most beautiful, being trained for both power and speed events. For men in their prime, beauty belongs to those prepared for the toils of active service: such types are good-looking and awe-inspiring at the same time. As for the old man, beauty here means being physically able to deal with inevitable tasks, and not be a nuisance to others . . .

That Aristotle identifies the pentathlete as most likely to exhibit aesthetic perfection of bodily form is not surprising. Already by the late fifth century BC, the disproportionate physical development brought on by certain sporting specializations was a subject for comment. In Xenophon's *Symposium*, for example, Socrates mentions the lanky and bulky figures cut respectively by long-distance runners and boxers (2.17). And we have already noted the statue-type created as a canonical ideal by Polykleitos: it was a 'Spear-Carrier', which means that if it represents an athlete, it must be a pentathlete, because javelin-throwing existed in games only as part of the pentathlon. But whatever the aesthetic premium attached to the pentathlete as a model of all-round physical symmetry, Aristotle reminds us of a radical factor in making such evaluations. The youth, the mature man, the old man: what is decisive in assessing beauty in each case is the apparent capacity of the body to withstand exertion, hardship, and above all *ponos*. And we have already seen what *ponos* implies: not the heavy labour of industrial activity, rather the struggle and suffering of frontline fighting. Aficionados of modern gym culture may blandly echo this ideal when they cite the litany of 'no pain, no gain'. In Classical antiquity, the gymnasium was both schooling and stand-by for the toils to be encountered on the battlefield. If not that, then, of course, there were the regular and multiple opportunities for agony in the stadium.

3

THE PROGRAMME OF AGONY

E arly in the fifth century BC the poet Pindar could salute Olympia as the 'pinnacle of contests' (*Olympian* 2.13). This salutation not only evokes the particularly gruelling levels of exertion demanded of Olympic participants. It also implies that there were other regular festivals for which athletes could prepare themselves. By the late sixth century, in fact, a calendar of competitive meetings was firmly established in the Greek-speaking world. This calendar became so busy as to foster, eventually, a breed of 'full-time' or professional sportsmen – athletes who could proceed from one occasion to the next, gathering prizes as they went. Many city-states held their own contests, often organized through the offices of the civic gymnasium, and usually staged under the auspices of a presiding deity. The Panathenaic Games, instituted at Athens after 566 BC, were the most

eminent of such local events. Both at the 'Greater' Panathenaia (held over four days every four years) and at the
'Lesser' Panathenaia (a two-day ritual, celebrated annually) there were various equestrian and physical events in
honour of Athena. But even the prestige of the Panathenaic Games was overshadowed by the principal 'circuit',
or *periodos*, of four 'Sacred and Crown Games', as they
later came to be called: the quadrennial meetings convened at the sanctuaries of Olympia and Delphi, and the
biennial celebrations at Isthmia and Nemea.

The festival at Delphi was known as the Pythian
Games. According to legend it developed as a primarily
musical thanksgiving for the god Apollo's victory over a
dragon, the Python, and Apollo's subsequent claim on
oracular power at the remote and mountainous site. A
Greek historical inscription, however, relates that athletics at Delphi began in 590 BC with an *agôn gymnikos
chrêmatites* – a 'gymnastic contest for money', funded
from war booty – then reinvented itself as an *agôn steph-
anitês*, or 'Crown Games', in 582 BC. In any case, while
Olympia provided a model for purely symbolic prizes
and select athletic disciplines, Delphi nurtured its special
reputation for choral and instrumental excellence. Lyre-
playing, poetic recitation, the pipes – these enjoyed the
divine patronage of Apollo no less than running, boxing,
or chariot-driving.

The year 582 BC is also the date assigned for the
beginning of the Isthmian Games. Sponsored by the city
of Corinth, ostensibly in memory of the infant hero

Melikertes – whose body was brought to the Corinthian shore, so legend went, by dolphins – the biennial gatherings at Isthmia came under the divine presidency of Poseidon. That they were modelled on the pattern set by Olympia is very likely: the late seventh-century tyrant of Corinth, Kypselos, made dedications at Olympia, including a remarkable carved and inlaid wooden chest that was displayed for many centuries in the Temple of Hera (described in detail by Pausanias: 5.17.5 onwards). There was some political tension between the respective organizers of the Olympian and Isthmian Games, but the geographical location of Isthmia – accessible by sea from east and west – made it well placed to uphold the main common principle of the Sacred and Crown Games, to be open to all Greeks. This 'all-Greek', or Panhellenic, status was not quite as generous as it sounds, with various categories of Greek-speaking people being firmly excluded from joining the ceremonies and competitions. But the pre-eminence of the Olympia-Delphi-Isthmia-Nemea *periodos* was largely established by virtue of this Panhellenic ethos. Even after the Greek city-states had succumbed to conquest first by the Macedonians and then the Romans, the four festivals continued to attract athletes and pilgrims from a wide area around the Mediterranean basin, and Greek continued to serve as the common language of the gatherings.

Fifty years ago it would have been reasonable to say that the Nemean Games, instituted in 573 BC, were the most obscure of the Panhellenic quartet. But excavations undertaken by the University of California since 1974 have steadily illuminated the site, which is located in the northeast Peloponnese. Kleonai is the city-state historically credited with raising the status of Nemea, mythically derived from funeral games held in honour of a local hero called Opheltes, who died from a snake-bite while only an infant. That myth connects to the more widely known saga of 'The Seven Against Thebes'; and not far from Nemea lies Mycenae, the citadel-base of Homer's mighty Agamemnon. But probably no story was more supportive of Nemea's reputation abroad than the tale of Herakles and the Nemean Lion.

This was one of the 'Labours' of Herakles imposed on the hero by King Eurystheus of Tiryns. Herakles, in a frenzy of madness, had murdered his wife and children. To expiate this crime, he was ordered (by the oracle at Delphi) to submit to a series of dangerous, distasteful, or near-suicidal tasks as stipulated by Eurystheus. The Greek word for these punishments was *athla*. Over time, a dozen of them became particularly well known, forming a sequence of 'Twelve Labours', or *dodekathlon*. This 'canonical' selection of mythical episodes may have come about directly as a result of the building of the Temple of Zeus at Olympia *c.*460 BC, where the architectural embellishment allowed for six sculpted panels (metopes) to feature above the columns at either end (see Fig. 37). So certain Labours had to be chosen, and it has been plausibly suggested that the choice may have been made with Panhellenic considerations in mind – that is, to represent deeds of Herakles located in various parts of the world as the Greeks knew it, not just the mainland of Greece. First of all, however, came the hero's struggle with a lion that had been terrorizing Nemea. This lion had an impenetrable pelt: so Herakles had to approach at close quarters, and dispatch the beast with a stranglehold or wrestling-throw (**Fig. 13**).

The salutation to *Herakles Kallinikos*, perhaps best translated as 'Herakles the Conqueror', occurs in early Greek poetry of the mid-seventh century BC and echoes down the years of emulative sport in Classical antiquity. The imitation of Herakles at Olympia and elsewhere could go to extraordinary lengths: the most bizarre tale concerns a Cynic philosopher who in AD 168 dressed himself up as the hero and died likewise – by setting his shirt on fire (Lucian, *On the End of Peregrinus* 36). But there was a sense in which *every* Classical male athlete strove to be a second Herakles, undertaking to train and compete as if facing up to the trials of nightmarish persecution by one monster after another. Greek parlance acknowledged this by letting the noun *athlon* (or *athlos*) connote any sort of fight or contest; with the verb *athleuo* meaning not only 'I take part in a contest' but 'I suffer'. On the positive side, the same cognate term implies that such suffering is not for nothing: with *athlos* also meaning 'prize', the expectation of reward is firmly attached. So Herakles, at the end of his hard-fought and much-suffering life, gained the greatest prize of all – elevation to immortal rank, joining the Olympian gods.

13. Herakles versus the Nemean Lion: detail of an Athenian red-figure amphora attributed to the Andokides Painter, *c.*520 BC.

In this virtuous spirit, ideally, an athlete dedicated himself to the hours of practice and conditioning at the gymnasium. Now it is time for us to examine what happened after the training – to trace the schedules of agony that awaited those who entered Olympia as 'the peak of contests'.

The Scrutiny

The earliest athletic ceremonies at Olympia were local affairs: not until the sixth or fifth century BC did the festival become self-consciously Panhellenic. Aside from the entry restrictions of gender, ethnicity, and social rank, however, it is clear that even the Panhellenic Olympic Games were by no means open to all. All intending competitors were subject to official scrutiny. Those who did not meet certain standards were sent home.

When Pausanias visited Olympia in the mid-second century AD, it was obligatory for athletes to present themselves at the sanctuary – or to the satellite city of Elis, where training facilities were more extensive – a full month before competition started. Only drastic excuses for late arrival, such as shipwreck *en route*, were accepted. This particular stipulation can only have come into force after the lapsing of the tradition of a 'Sacred Truce' (by which cessation of hostilities around the Greek world was ensured for the duration of the Olympic festival). Since the scrutiny served primarily to ensure the quality of the competition, it may have been introduced during the fourth century BC, when athletes began arriving from further afield. (As for the 'Sacred Truce', it can have been no more than a formality after the second century BC, when the ideology of Roman rule (*pax Romana*) was established around the Mediterranean and beyond, making any further 'pacifism' redundant.)

So along with the protocols of religious oath-taking there developed a thorough system of screening and seeding all competitors. The officials appointed to supervise this scrutiny were known as the *Hellanodikai* – literally, 'Greek judges', or 'judges of the Greeks'. Selected specially for each Olympiad, they formed a 'college' of adjudicators, eventually up to twelve in number, whose sign of office was a florid purple cloak. Their responsibilities included the conduct of various purificatory rites, the refereeing of events, the levying of fines for offences, and the assignment of prizes. Once all entrants were assembled and training together in the precincts of Olympia or Elis, the *Hellanodikai* also had proper opportunity to assess relative levels of fitness and ability, and to match opponents accordingly. In theory, this should have ensured better entertainment when the spectators arrived – or, at least, fewer one-sided contests. The period of surveillance may also have served to deter the use of any performance-enhancing tricks or drugs.

No-hopers, evidently, were weeded out at this stage. One ancient author (Philostratos, *Life of Apollonius* 5.43) reports the wording of a stern exhortation that was issued by the *Hellanodikai* to athletes on the eve of the Games. *'You who have worked hard enough to qualify for Olympia, ridding from your lives whatever is idle and cowardly – proceed. Those who have not trained themselves to this level – let them wander where they please.'*

Taking Oaths and Drawing Lots

All those participating in the Olympic Games – the adult athletes and their trainers, the boys and their guardians, and the judges too – were required to take an oath before activities commenced. We do not know the exact wording of this pledge – it is only reported in paraphrase by Pausanias (5.24.9–10) – but it seems to have been a solemn formality, conducted by the Council House to the south of the Temple of Zeus, and in the presence of an awe-inducing statue of Zeus brandishing thunderbolts in each hand. This form of Zeus was known as *Zeus Horkios*, 'Zeus of Oaths', and at an altar in front of the god's image the sacrifice was made of a wild boar. Over chunks of roasted boar, athletes and their guardians would vouchsafe that they had been in training for the past ten months; furthermore, that they would do nothing to bring the Games into disrepute. For their part, the judges promised to do their duties fairly, and not to accept any bribes. The overseeing of this procedure, and other sacrifices in the course of the festival, was principally devolved to three senior *theokoloi*, or 'servants of the god': unlike the long-term 'seers' at Olympia (see p. 175), these priests were elected, and served by rotation. (Their residential headquarters were at the 'Theokoleion', located south of the *palaistra*; inscriptions make it clear that a host of subordinates, including designated wood-choppers, were also involved.)

Previous to the tradition of a month-long residency, there seems to have been a more cursory process at Olympia which the Greeks referred to as a 'parade' or 'scrutiny' (*dokimasia*). Athletes lined up before the judges for various checks – an important one being whether they should compete among the men (*andres*) or the boys (*paides*) – and horses, too, were inspected for their age and condition. Some basic order may have been imposed at this stage concerning various categories of size, experience, and suchlike. But ultimately the business of assigning the order of bouts, heats, and lanes for racing was down to chance. It was done by a drawing of lots, or sortition – in Greek, a *klêros*. We have a clear description of how this operated for the combat events such as wrestling or boxing. The competitors gathered in a circle, and an urn was passed around. In the urn were as many tokens as there were competitors, each token inscribed with a letter of the alphabet, and each token making part of a pair – two tokens marked *alpha*, two marked *beta*, and so on. (Alternatively, a shard etched with a letter was broken in half, to be reunited by the lottery.) As the urn went round, everyone took a token. So the fighter who pulled out an *alpha* would be drawn against the fighter who picked the next *alpha* (or matching segment). If an odd number of contestants was assembled, the lucky one getting a bye into the next round was whoever at the end had no matching token.

Participants in this selection process might take some heart from a statue group that could be seen close to the Temple of Zeus. As noted by Pausanias (5.25.8), this showed a set of Achaean (legendary Greek) heroes conducting a similar process. It was an episode in the Trojan War, as relayed in Book 7 of Homer's *Iliad*: with the specific business being to decide which of the nine Greek chieftains besieging Troy should meet the challenge of a duel with the Trojan champion, Hector. The imposing bronze heroes were ranged in an arc, awaiting the result, while old Nestor stood apart as umpire, shaking the lots in an upturned helmet.

The sculptor of this group – which was raised a little before *c.*460 BC – was Onatas from Aegina, who also made a number of victory statues at Olympia. Some scholars have speculated that two statues recovered off the coast of Italy, the so-called 'Riace Bronzes' (Fig. 14), were once part of the assemblage. Their poses and demeanours are certainly appropriate. In any case, it is not fanciful to imagine that this group effectively heroized the practice of drawing lots at Olympia. The nudity of the epic Achaeans on their pedestals reflected another feature of the *klêros* procedure, which was that competitors stripped off for the occasion. Like the weigh-in before a modern boxing match, this offered the chance to intimidate one's prospective opponents. In the exemplary drawing of lots among Homer's heroes, the

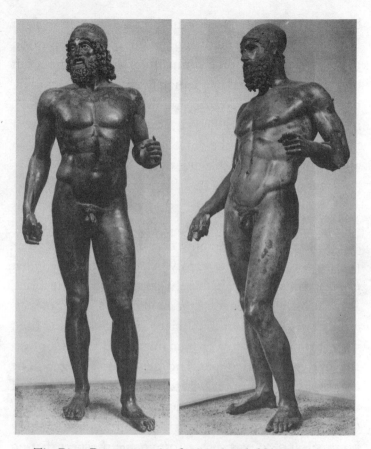

14. The Riace Bronzes: a pair of original mid-fifth century
BC statues probably exported from Greece towards Italy
in antiquity. Slightly over life-size, and undoubtedly
heroic, the bronzes may have belonged to a larger group,
but there is no consensus regarding their provenance or
authorship.

brawny Ajax is overjoyed to find himself chosen to fight Hector. But inscriptions from the Graeco-Roman world make it clear that some competitors digested the result of the first draw and immediately withdrew. According to the attestation of Marcus Aurelius Asclepiades (p. 167), no secret was made of how often a prospective opponent has scratched from the outset or a contest come to an abrupt halt after the drawing of lots.

Pausanias mentions an athlete from Alexandria who, at Olympiad 201 (of AD 25), took one look at his opponents and ran away (5.21.18). But Pausanias also states that this was the only occasion on which a competitor was fined for cowardly behaviour. In the combat events, as we shall see, there were no weight categories. It must have happened often enough that some colossus appeared whom no normal-sized individual in his right mind would dream of challenging. Such discretion was the better part of valour, and generally indulged. The epigraphy of champion fighters even makes a virtue of the number of times that victory was gained 'dustless' (*akoniti*): meaning that when he presented himself for a bout, so-and-so was such a formidable prospect that no one would confront him – so he never needed to dust for action.

The Early 'Olympic Village'

All ancient accounts agree on this: that part of the agony involved in the ancient Olympics was simply being there.

The seasonal timing of the festival alone was enough to make it unpleasant for all concerned. The precise dates were not absolutely fixed, but seem to have been reckoned around the first full moon after the summer solstice, meaning that the games were usually staged in what we would term mid-August. This is just the time of year when most Greeks nowadays like to escape to the seaside, with good reason: for on coastline and islands fierce sunshine comes with a freshening breeze. Inland places such as Olympia can become unbearably hot. And that is how it was when the athletes and spectators converged for this great sporting occasion – an over-heated, land-locked valley, blighted by flies and dust, which for centuries offered hardly anything in the way of 'public conveniences' or 'comfort zones'.

Public toilets were not provided at Olympia until the late first century AD, by which time when the sanctuary had come firmly under Roman imperial administration. There was a long-established practice of sinking temporary well-shafts to supply extra water while the festival took place. But the water-basin terraced into the north side of the Altis was engineered only in AD 141–57, thanks to a benefaction from Herodes Atticus. Depending upon a Roman-style aqueduct running down a distance of several kilometres from springs by the hilltop village of Miraka, this cleared certain endemic diseases from the site, and cooled outbreaks of collective bad temper among Olympic spectators (Lucian, *On the End of Peregrinus* 19).

In the mid-fourth century BC a well-meaning man called Leonidas, from the island of Naxos, had set the precedent for individuals 'enhancing' Olympia with improved visitor facilities: Leonidas endowed, and perhaps also designed, the expansive colonnaded hostel and banqueting pavilion that stood by the southwest corner of the Altis. Macedonians and Romans made further substantial improvements to Olympia's monumental appearance and infrastructure. But otherwise the normal Olympic sojourn was a notoriously squalid experience for athletes and spectators alike. Illustrious figures travelling to Olympia from all around the Mediterranean were expected to pitch camp or sleep rough in fields between the sanctuary and the two rivers flowing nearby. At best the resulting 'Olympic village' must have resembled a shanty town of tents, dens, and improvised wooden shacks, with food and other necessities on sale from numerous hawkers – doubtless charging extortionate prices. Public order was maintained by cohorts of specially hired policemen whose on-the-spot mode of keeping control is denoted by references to them as 'whip-bearers' (*mastigophoroi*).

The high summer scenario can be all too vividly imagined. Epictetus, the Greek philosopher who did so much to spread the doctrine of Stoicism or 'long-sufferance' in the first century AD, could use Olympia as a byword for persistent inconvenience and unpleasantness in human experience – overcrowded, under-equipped, made bearable only by the quality of the spectacle (*Discourses* 1.6.27–8). Another Classical writer reports that the most effective way of dealing with disobedient slaves was to threaten to send them to watch the Olympic Games: it was worse than working a treadmill (Aelian, *Varia Historia* 14.18).

The Timetable of Events

After the preliminaries of the Olympic festival, those athletes not already stricken by dysentery or dehydration were tested by a timetable of competitive activity that was brief, intense, and exhausting. It lasted just three days. Although it was, for something like a thousand years, a fairly consistent timetable, we cannot reconstruct its structure with perfect accuracy. However, the following order of events is generally agreed: first, chariot-racing and other equestrian contests; second, the pentathlon; third, the various foot-races; then the so-called 'heavy contests' of wrestling, boxing, and *pankration*; finally, the race in armour. It seems that a separate day was set aside for all the boys' competitions; and throughout the programme were also interspersed further sacred rites and processions, a grand banquet for all participants, and of course a prize-giving ceremony.

Keeping to the above order of events, we can now add some details regarding their nature and expectations, including in this survey character sketches of some ancient sporting 'celebrities'.

CHARIOT-RACING

Chariot-racing was certainly the most prestigious contest of the Olympic Games, and probably the most exciting to watch: yet it immediately presents us with an ideological puzzle. The ancient Olympics, we have argued, were quintessentially about striving for victory by dint of personal effort. Yet the Olympic event with most at stake was also the only event in which the winner usually did nothing at all. He provided the horses and the chariot, and he hired a driver. If his team were successful, then it was the owner who took the crown. (Or, we should add, *her* team – since in the early fourth century BC Kyniska, a Spartan princess, became the first of several women to gain Olympic victory in this event: see Pausanias 3.8.1 and *IvO* 160).

This exception to the general laws of Olympic justice must be understood by reference to the particularly aristocratic status of equestrian pursuits. Horse-ownership and horse-display were defining aspects of high rank in Greek society since at least the eighth century BC. To judge from the early bronze votives found at Olympia, some form of equine trialling was practised in the vicinity before the formal institution of the Games; and the east pediment of the Temple of Zeus makes a chariot-race part of the sanctuary's mythical basis. Social distinction, however, is what underpins the archaeology and mythology of charioteering at Olympia. There are images and relics of chariot-driving from 'princely' tombs of the Mycenaean period in the Peloponnese; and as we have seen, Homer's account of chariot-racing at the funeral games of Patroklos (*Iliad* 23. 262–650) suggests that no contest mattered more to the Greek chieftains at Troy.

So in the late fifth century BC – probably at the meeting of 416 BC – one wealthy and flamboyant Athenian signalled his ambitions for political and military power when he entered no fewer than seven chariot teams at Olympia, multiplying his chances of gaining the crown. This was Alcibiades, the friend and would-be lover of Socrates, and he gained, it seems, first, second, and fourth places (Thucydides 6.16). The victory list for the chariot events is dominated by individuals who feature in the chronicles of ancient history as tyrants or kings; and ultimately, we cannot be surprised to learn what happened in the year AD 67, when the Roman emperor Nero took part in a special contest for ten-horse chariots. Nero had not much experience of chariots; he fell off, and failed to finish the race. Yet he was awarded victory; for which, we are told, he reimbursed the race officials handsomely (Suetonius, *Life of Nero* 24).

Chariot-racing at Olympia took place in a rectangular area called the Hippodrome to the south of the Stadium. Since washed away by the floodwaters of the Alpheios, the Hippodrome was also where other horse-and-jockey races were organized – bareback riding and without stirrups – plus, for a certain period in the fifth century BC, cart-races with mules. But the prime attraction was the four-horse chariot-race, or *tethrippon*, established in 680 BC at the 25th Olympiad. Around forty chariots might be entered for what was an arduous test of a driver's skill and his horses' stamina. The chariots were light, two-wheeled vehicles, with room for just one steersman, who wore long robes (**Fig. 15**). A pair of horses ran under a central yoke, with flanking steeds attached by harness. There was a staggered order for starting – again, lots were cast to determine the initial line-up – and an early fifth-century BC sculptor called Kleoitas boasts about having devised ingenious starting-gates (Pausanias 6.20.14); but since the race went for a distance of something like nine miles, there was time over the course for adroit teams to assert themselves. Twelve double laps of the Hippodrome were required, therefore involving twenty-four hairpin turns. Mishaps at the turn-ing-point (*nyssa*) were common, often serious. This was an event that left contestants ecstatic if they won – and probably grateful if they simply made it to the finish.

How often did the owner of a chariot-team take the reins for the race? Apart from 'very rarely', no accurate answer can be given to that question. But it is worth mentioning here one attractive theory devised to explain the nature of a powerful statue discovered not long ago on the island of Motya, off the southern tip of Italy (**Fig. 16**). Unlike the so-called 'Delphi Charioteer' – part of a coeval victory-monument in hollow bronze – the Motya charioteer's robe clings to his body, emphasizing his musculature. Here are the pronounced contours of a typically prize-winning, *palaistra*-honed body. So the

15. The Delphi Charioteer: part of a bronze chariot-group
dedicated at Delphi after 480 BC by Polyzalos, tyrant of Gela.
Height 1.80 m.

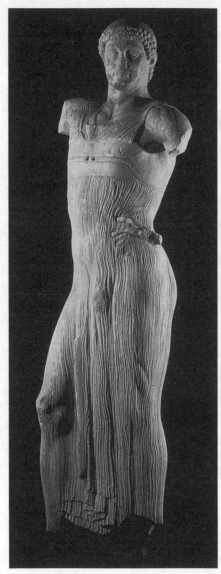

16. The Motya
Charioteer: marble
statue of *c*.470 BC.
Height 1.81 m.

piece may be intended to distinguish its subject as not merely a hired driver, but a well-to-do member of the gymnastic and equestrian aristocracy.

PENTATHLON

Literally, the 'five-fold challenge', the pentathlon included the following series of disciplines: running, jumping, discus-throw, javelin-throw, and wrestling. Two of these events – the running and the wrestling – were also staged as contests in their own right, and we shall consider them as such separately. The remaining three occurred only as part of the pentathlon: which means, incidentally, that every Classical statue of a discus-thrower is effectively the image of a pentathlete. Of all ancient athletes, the pentathlete was the one who could claim to be an 'all-rounder', and was therefore the physical type most likely to exhibit balance, symmetry, and measured proportions – qualities esteemed by ancient Greek artists, physiologists, and philosophers alike.

The sequence of events within the pentathlon is debated. It is likely that competition commenced with running, and that this was a sprint race over the length of the stadium (about 200 metres). It is also likely that the wrestling came as a finale – and a finale that was not contested, if a winner had already emerged. Again this is a matter for dispute, but the scoring system for the pentathlon evidently worked along the same principle as a men's tennis match today, that is 'best of five'. Once a contestant had three outright victories, then it was futile to waste energy on the remaining disciplines. We cannot be sure if second-place outcomes contributed to the rankings. It does seem clear, however, that a process of elimination occurred. If after four events the overall winner had not yet been decided – say two athletes had two victories apiece – then the ultimate event was a decider, restricted to those in position to take the crown with a third win.

The discus began as a stone platter and evolved into bronze or iron. Neither its weight nor diameter had standard calibrations: in a given contest, athletes were obliged to use the largest implement that one of their number had brought along. The average weight of sur-viving Greek *diskoi* is around 2 kg (4.4 lbs), like the men's discus today, though one iron discus has been found (at Nemea) weighing over 8 kg (17.6 lbs), bring-ing to mind a story to be found in the Latin epic poet Statius, where at the first Nemean Games an athlete called Hippomedon brings along a discus so huge that most of his rivals immediately retire (*Thebaid* 6.646 ff.). As for the throwing technique, there was no rangy rotational movement as shown by modern discus-throwers: rather, the disc was launched from a fixed-feet position on a platform or low podium (called a *balbis*), with centrifugal force generated by flexing the knees and twisting the trunk **(Fig. 17)**. The torsion demanded by this ancient style of *diskobolia* is almost impossibly con-veyed by the statue-type created in the mid-fifth century BC by Myron, and much beloved by the Romans **(Fig. 18)**. Distances were marked by wooden pegs; and

17. Rear view of the discus-throw: fragment of an Athenian red-figure oil-flask (*alabastron*) attributed to Onesimos, *c.*490 BC. Length 13.4 cm.

18. 'Lancellotti Discobolus': marble copy made *c.* AD 140 after a
bronze original by Myron *c.*460–450 BC. Height 1.55 m.
Discovered on Rome's Esquiline Hill in 1781, the statue was
controversially acquired by Adolf Hitler in 1938, being
returned to Italy ten years later.

because no safety nets or 'cages' were erected, it is perhaps not surprising that several Greek myths relate instances of accidental death-by-discus to a bystander.

How jumps were performed is less apparent. There was a take-off board; and we know that athletes gained extra forward momentum by swinging metal dumb-bells, or *haltêres*, in their hands (again, the weight of these objects was not standardized: examples have been found varying between 2 and 4.5 kg). But the challenge was not a single leap for height, nor a single leap for length. An epigram about a fifth-century BC champion pentathlete and distinguished soldier called Phayllos records a distance of over 50 feet, or 16 metres − roughly double the sort of length to which an international long-jumper of today would aspire. If this is an accurate measurement, then how was it achieved? A sequence of bounds is probable, perhaps something like the modern triple-jump, although a plausible case has been made for there to have been five leaps, not three. In any case, final landing was generally made in a sandpit. The custom of doing such successive jumps with fists closed around small dumb-bells certainly made the event a good test of explosive reflexes and (in the jargon of modern sports physiology) plyometric strength (**Fig. 19**).

The javelin is usually regarded as the athletic event with closest relevance to ancient military practice. However, as part of the pentathlon the javelin-throw (*akontismos*) departed from the practicalities of the battlefield in one key respect. It was a test of distance:

19. Athletic scenes on an Athenian red-figure drinking-cup, c.480 BC: in the centre, a youth practising with jumping-weights.

there was no target to aim for, as would be the case in hoplite training. Hoplites did not throw javelins; they thrust their spears at the enemy, using a stout shaft of cornel wood. Because absolute distance was what mattered to the athletes, the javelin was modified to assist its aerodynamic properties. Shaped from light elder wood and tipped with metal, it was partly bound up by a loose cord which the thrower used to give extra pull and spin on the shaft at the time of release. Vase paintings show that the javelin was held between middle and fore finger: with the cord looped onto one or both fingers, the thrower took a few steps forward, extended his throwing arm, and then literally unleashed the javelin on an upward trajectory (**Fig. 20**). The rotary motion imparted by the untwisting cord would keep the spear aloft for longer, and travelling perhaps to a distance of well over 100 metres.

One further comment should be made about the pentathlon. Vases that depict throwing and jumping frequently indicate that these exercises were performed to the musical accompaniment of the double-pipes. So not only was the pentathlon suited to the physically versatile; it promoted the union of rhythm and effort. It is true that pipers once accompanied Greek foot-soldiers into combat, a practice which the Spartans maintained (see Thucydides 5.70); but here the flute tunes were not so much played to raise adrenalin levels, rather they seem to anticipate an axiom of modern coaching wisdom – that the athlete who is relaxed and at ease can produce better results than one straining with sheer all-out effort.

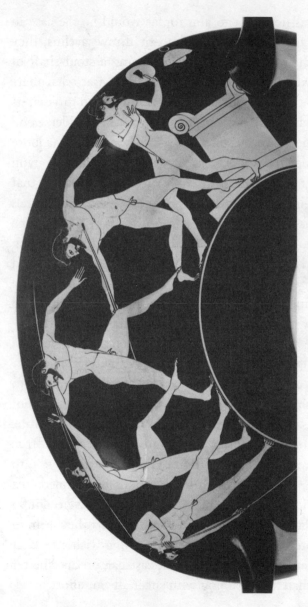

20. The javelin-throw: detail of an Athenian red-figure cup attributed to the Carpenter Painter, c.515–510 BC.

WRESTLING

As etymology indicates, wrestling (*palê*) was the principal activity of the *palaistra*, and a much more widely practised sport in antiquity than it is in the modern world – where judo, kung-fu, and karate are preferred. 'Ground wrestling' (*katô palê*) – probably freestyle grappling and rolling around in the sandpit of the *palaistra* – was usually distinguished from the 'upright wrestling' (*orthôs palê*) commonly depicted on Greek vases. Combatants circled around, each looking for an initial clutch to the wrists or neck of his opponent; guile and experience could count for more than brute force, in a contest where victory went to whoever got the best of five bouts. There were no timed rounds: a bout ended when a throw was made which had its victim prone on the ground. Three throws, then, signified victory (*triaktêr*, 'three-timer', generically entered Greek parlance as 'winner'). An elementary ring may have been erected at Olympia: it seems that wrestling, and other combat events, could take place in the Altis itself, with spectators crowding along the Echo Colonnade and up the lower slopes of the Hill of Kronos. Points were not awarded, but referees stood by with rods to enforce the rules.

What were the rules? Pausanias (6.4.3) mentions an athlete from Sicily who wrestled successfully at Olympia by the blunt strategy of breaking his opponents' fingers; but fragments of an inscribed bronze plaque from Olympia, datable to the late sixth century BC, contain a regulation explicitly forbidding such deliberate injury to the fingers. To judge by numerous ancient literary references, and some surviving excerpts from a wrestling manual, this was a discipline that had a complex science and jargon of its own. Only categories of age, not size, were recognized: but as it is an encounter in which throws might be accomplished by grabbing an opponent by the knees, or tripping him at the ankles, wrestling offered some chance for the nimble fighter to bring down a hulk. Celebrity wrestlers, however, tended towards the gigantic, and the most notorious was perhaps the semi-legendary Milo of Croton.

Victor in the boys' wrestling at Olympia probably in 540 BC, Milo went on to gather multiple accolades from the Panhellenic circuit, including five further triumphs at Olympia, perhaps more (see p. 160) – so he must have been a successful wrestler into at least his late thirties. He was only thwarted from a seventh Olympic title by a young opponent from his home town who was a pioneer of the technique of *akrocheirismos* – literally 'high-handedness', effectively wrestling at arm's length – and who thereby avoided a rib-cracking embrace.

Numerous ancient anecdotes survive attesting the enormous capacity of both Milo's muscles and his appetite; some also remark on the diminutive size of his brain. Allegedly his end came when he was in a forest and came across a tree that woodcutters had tried to split, leaving wedges driven into its trunk. Milo could not resist trying to finish the job. He parted the trunk enough for the wedges to drop out – but then the wood and pith closed in on his fingers, trapping him there, to be gnawed alive by a pack of wolves. Like all Milo stories, this seems like fable. But distinguishing myth from reality was not of great concern to most ancient Greeks. So we may recall that when Milo entered battle on behalf of Croton, against the neighbouring state of Sybaris, in 510 BC, he did so not only displaying his crowns of Olympic victory, but also dressed up like Herakles, with lionskin cloak and knotty club. Herakles himself had been tested on his wrestling skills: apart from the Nemean Lion, for instance, there was the story of Antaios, a giant who relied for his strength upon contact with Mother Earth – so had to be lifted off the ground by Herakles in order to be defeated (**Fig. 21**).

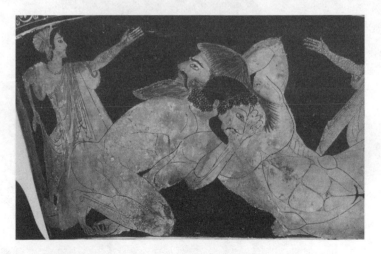

21. Herakles versus Antaios: detail of an Athenian red-figure calyx-krater by Euphronios, *c.*520–510 BC.

22. Bronze statuette of wrestlers; of the third century BC. Height 14 cm. The bearded figure may be intended as Herakles.

But practitioners of all the ancient combat sports were, as we have noted, striving to be successors of Herakles. (When covered in oil and dust, they may even have appeared like the first mortals of Greek mythology – the prototype figures of wet clay fashioned by Prometheus.)

Modern popular wrestling has become a sort of knockabout farce, scarcely illuminating its ancient appeal. But a series of statue groups produced in the early Hellenistic period goes some way towards conveying the sport's original excitement **(Fig. 22)**.

BOXING

There were no weight categories in ancient boxing, so this was a sport which clearly favoured the hefty. Both Greek (*pygmê*) and Latin (*pugillare*) words for boxing imply use of the fists; and since no padded gloves were worn for a bout, only tightly wrapped leather thongs, serious damage might be inflicted, especially about the face and ears. The bronze head of a boxer recovered from Olympia **(Fig. 23)** displays the troughs and corrugations of a face repeatedly hit hard; in Hellenistic sculpture such portraits of fighters seem almost like a type of theatrical mask. As if this were not enough, boxers in Roman times are alleged to have added metal studs to their fist-bindings, producing the *caestus* – more of a knuckleduster than a glove.

Could any boxer remain intact? It seems unlikely, but perhaps the case of Melancomas should be mentioned here. Melancomas is the name of a boxer fulsomely

23. Bronze head of a boxer from Olympia, perhaps Satyros of Elis, by Silanion, *c.*330 BC.

praised in two speeches by the distinguished Greek orator Dio Chrysostom ('Dio the Golden-mouthed'). Melancomas, from Caria on the coast of Asia Minor, was an Olympic victor in boxing during the first century AD: but to look at him, says Dio, you would have thought he was a runner – because he carried none of the scars of a pugilist's career. He took part in plenty of bouts, some of which went on all day: yet he remained not only undefeated but also unmarked. As a young man

Melancomas was 'very big and beautiful' – and he stayed that way.

Dio's eulogy of Melancomas (in *Orationes* 28 and 29) tends to exaggeration, but shows technical insight too. Ancient boxing was not limited by timekeepers and bells, so it tested stamina; and the absence of padded gloves gave fighters all the more reason to dodge each other's blows. Melancomas, it seems, was a virtuoso at dancing around his opponents and ducking their punches, until they simply gave up or collapsed. Part of his training schedule was to hold his arms up, extended, for long periods of time (up to two days, claims Dio). It was a strategy based on high-minded principles. 'Often,' declares Dio, 'he fought over an entire day at the hottest time of the year, and had the chance to end the fight, but opted not to. For he believed that sometimes an inept slugger can bring down the most skilful boxer with one erratic punch; whereas true victory, as he saw it, lay in forcing his opponents to surrender unbloodied. That meant they were yielding not to wounds but to themselves' (*Oratio* 29.12).

PANKRATION

The example of Melancomas may soften our view of the violence inherent in ancient boxing. But it is hard to find any mitigating evidence for the so-called *pankration*, which translates literally as 'the all-power thing', or 'total force'; more idiomatically, perhaps, as 'no holds barred'. To say that any kind of violence was permissible in this contest is not quite true: umpires were supposed to penalize biting and the gouging-out of eyes. But to kick, strangle, smite, and otherwise beat one's opponent into submission or death was a highly esteemed art, and some statues of prize-winning pankratiasts were venerated as magical touchstones of strength and healing powers.

Yet the best-known surviving image of this discipline does not commemorate an individual, nor even mark a victory. It is a marble ensemble discovered in Rome in 1583, and one which has served as a model of Classical athleticism for centuries (**Fig. 24**). However famous as an *objet d'art*, here we have two fighters who are entirely anonymous. Not only that, but they seem caught in a moment of fine equilibrium, a momentary *impasse*. Connoisseurs of ancient combat sports may argue that this group represents a decisive moment of the *pankration*. But to all other viewers, it remains uncertain who will win this bout. Is the figure on top about to be rolled over or thrown on his back? Is the figure below close to submission? Quite apart from the homoerotic suggestiveness of the piece, we are invited to guess the next move; so perhaps this 'entwining', or *symplegma* as the Greeks would call it, captures a typical point of suspense for onlookers.

To judge from its illustration on vases, the very refereeing of this sport could be drastic: if combatants had to be separated, it was done by thrashing at them with sticks. Again there were no timed bouts, but a single

24. The 'Wrestlers': marble group probably after a bronze original of *c.*300 BC. Height 0.89 m. The group has been read as representing the juncture of a *pankration* bout known as the *strebloun*, or 'straining' – as one fighter forces his opponent to the ground while twisting his arm behind him.

fight to the finish, which came with submission or surrender signalled by a hand gesture. Literary anecdotes and inscriptions alternate between telling us of contests that were over before they had even started (a hulk appears, and his opponent gives up immediately), and tussles that dredged for the deepest reserves of stamina and spirit.

The *pankration* seems to have entered the Olympic programme relatively late, over a century after the

traditional inaugural games of 776 BC. Mythically, however, the nature of the discipline was said to derive from
two heroic struggles – that of Theseus against the
Minotaur, and Herakles versus the Nemean Lion. The
Minotaur was a hybrid half-man, half-bull, which fed
upon human victims dropped into its haunt of a maze,
called the Labyrinth, on the island of Crete; while, as
already noted, the Nemean Lion was invulnerable, so
had to be attacked without weapons. Either way, these
tales served to validate the essentially ferocious scope of
the *pankration*; and helped to make demigods of the
sport's outstanding exponents. One such was a certain
Polydamas ('Many-subduing') from Skotoussa in Thessaly, who won the *pankration* at the 93rd Olympiad in
408 BC. Polydamas was, as Pausanias relates (6.5.1; see
also 7.27.6), 'the biggest man of his times'. Though he
failed to retain his Olympic title in the games of 404 BC,
he had already extended his reputation by other spectacular deeds. On the very slopes of Mount Olympus, he
subdued a lion with his bare hands, a feat he also demonstrated in Asia. Proving his mighty strength, he also
stopped a chariot going full tilt; and grasped onto a bull
that was bucking so vigorously that it snapped away,
leaving Polydamas still holding its hooves. Invited by
the Great King of Persia to do combat with the most
formidable of his royal bodyguards, the so-called
'Immortals', Polydamas took on three at once and laid
them all out dead. He met his own end by an act of self-
sacrifice. He was drinking in a grotto with some friends

when the ceiling of the cave began to fall in. Polydamas held up the roof so that his companions could escape, then it collapsed, burying him.

The base of a posthumous statue to Polydamas has been recovered from Olympia, and shows a figure wrestling down a lion; and a large head from Rome, complete with cauliflower ears, is thought to represent the athlete (Fig. 25). What did the rest of his body look like? Very

25. Marble head of first century AD, perhaps after a portrait of Polydamas by Lysippos c.340–330 BC.

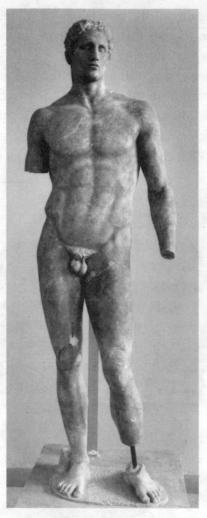

26. Marble statue of Agias at Delphi: replica of a bronze original
    by Lysippos, 337–336 BC. An accompanying inscription tells us
    that Agias (grandfather of Daochus II, co-ruler of Thessaly,
    who commissioned the work as part of an ancestral group)
    won the *pankration* once at the Olympic, three times at the
    Pythian, and five times at the Isthmian Games.

likely it was similar to another celebrated Thessalian pankratiast called Agias, who was commemorated in a statue group at Delphi **(Fig. 26)**. But the stories about Polydamas are enough to create a clear heroical alter-ego for posterity – going further than Milo of Croton in this mimetic game. As Pausanias saw, tackling a lion without weapons was a straight emulation of Herakles and the Nemean Lion. Wrestling with a bull, too, had its archetype in myth – both Herakles and Theseus had done likewise, not to mention the Minotaur – and as for taking on three Persian stalwarts at once, that was suggestive of Herakles raiding the triple-bodied monster called Geryon. As Herakles was a great pankratiast *manqué*, so a prize-winning pankratiast was of all athletes most eligible for heroization.

RUNNING

In the Olympic programme there were running races over various distances. The shortest, the *stade*, was a dash the length of the running track (*stadion*), which at Olympia measured 192 metres; then there was the 'double-furrow' (*diaulos*) up and down the stadium, going around a hairpin turning-point (*kamptêr*) at one end; with the furthest, bluntly known as the *dolichos*, 'the long one', entailing a number of stadium-lengths, sometimes as many as 24 (that is, approaching 5,000 metres), but more often around 12 (about a mile and a half, or 2,400 metres). Though the Greeks used the 'stade' as a routine unit of measurement, there appears to have been no absolutely standard length for athletic stadia (the stadium at Delphi measures 177 metres; that at Pergamon, 210 metres). In a sporting context, this hardly mattered, in so far as no timed records were kept: athletes ran not against the clock, but to confirm their relative superiority of pace. Running was a contest involving considerably less risk of personal injury than chariot-racing or the combat sports, but there is no evidence that it was therefore regarded with disdain. After all, the most lethal of participants in Homer's Trojan War was Achilles, whose usual Homeric epithet is 'fleet-footed' (*podarkes*), and whose swift efficiency as a killing-machine was in no small measure based upon his sprinting speed. In ancient Olympic annals, the stadium-length race was dignified as the elemental challenge, yielding the first recorded victor, Koroibos of Elis. And while physically they may have been more narrow-waisted than boxers or pankratiasts, the generic runners depicted upon Panathenaic prize vases do not present themselves as slight types. Bulging at the thighs and – like the short-distance champions of today – impressively pumped up around the biceps and upper body, they evidently combined a driving knee action with a punching, piston-like movement of the arms to gain extra momentum (**Fig. 27**) (though specialists in the *dolichos* were sensibly counselled to reserve that dynamic motion of 'sprint finish' until the last lap: see Philostratos, *On Gymnastics* 32).

Nothing like the modern 'marathon' was part of any ancient games. This seems odd, given that the event has

27. Sprinters on a Panathenaic prize amphora c.560–550 BC.
The scene is inscribed as *ANDRON STADIO* – 'the men's
stade-race'.

its origin in an episode of Classical history – albeit one that is often muddled in its retelling, and not consistent in the historical sources. There was a battle between Greeks and Persians at the site of Marathon in 490 BC: either a runner called Pheidippides (or Philippides) was dispatched from Athens to Sparta (some 160 miles) to fetch help, or a man called Eukles ran from Athens to Marathon to take part in the battle, and then ran back to give news of victory – an effort that cost him his life. In fact it was only for the first modern Olympics of 1896 that a course was mapped, from Marathon to Athens, and the 'marathon' distance subsequently fixed at just over 26 miles. Occasionally, in connection with religious festivals, certain ancient Greek cities did organize a sort of relay-race with torches. But what we should call 'long-distance' running was never countenanced as a sport – probably because 'day-running' was a regular or servile job devolved to full-time messengers and couriers.

Races in the stadium were bare-footed, over a surface of rolled sand. Contestants gathered at an inscribed starting-line, according to an order decided by lot (a good position at the start might help a runner avoid sharp elbows around the turning-post). At Olympia there was space for twenty at a time. At the starting-line a stone slab, grooves, or toe-holds were cut, providing both purchase for the first few strides and a strict equality in the line-up. At Isthmia, archaeology points to an ingenious wooden barrier or gate from which competitors were released at the pull of a cord, and there are several literary references to a mechanism or 'trap' that ensured no false starts. Something similar may have been in place at Olympia; if not, it seems the deterrent for premature departure was simply a whipping. The signal for off was a shout (*'Apite!'* – 'Away you go!') or a trumpet-blast. There may have been lanes marked out that runners were obliged to respect as they hared back and forth, and we surmise that the turning-post was elevated, lest anyone swing round it. All the same, barging, tripping, and general mishaps were probably routine – if the Roman poet Vergil's description of a foot-race between heroes (*Aeneid* 5. 315–39) is credible.

The *hoplitodromos*, or race in armour, at Olympia was a sprint over two lengths of the stadium. Introduced into the timetable at the 65th Olympiad of 520 BC, this event required athletes to wear helmets on their heads and metal greaves below the knees, and to compete while also carrying the large round shield that was the main protective device of the Greek infantry soldier, or hoplite. (Twenty-five such shields were kept in the Temple of Hera.) The rule about wearing greaves was later dropped; and running with a shield was a particularly artificial exercise, given that soldiers forming part of a hoplite troop in battle formation (the *phalanx*) were supposed to stay close together, with each man's shield overlapping to defend his immediate comrade. Nonetheless, this encumbered race was patently the most militaristic of all the athletic events at Olympia; it may even have been introduced precisely as a response to criticism that the agonistic programme had become too much of an end in itself. (Plutarch says that the event came last in the competitive sequence precisely in order to emphasize that the ultimate aim of athletics was military prowess: *Moralia* 639e.) Yet the *hoplitodromos* as a

28. Interior of an Athenian red-figure drinking cup (*kylix*) attributed to the Colmar Painter, *c*.480 BC, showing a prize-winning competitor in the *hoplitodromos*. The words painted by his shield declare *HO PAIS KALOS* – 'The beautiful boy'.

contest could never serve to strengthen *esprit de corps*. A single competitor had always to triumph – and be celebrated like any other winner (Fig. 28).

Games for Girls

When the Olympics were 'revived' in the nineteenth century, it was taken for granted that women would not compete. This exclusion was not modelled on any ancient ideal; merely based on prevailing gender stereotypes, and the widespread exclusion of women from political, military, and financial affairs. If we bear in mind that female competitors were firmly excluded from the first modern Olympics of 1896, and only gradually gained entry to the track and field programme at subsequent Olympiads, beyond such 'gentle' exertions as tennis, archery, and swimming (a separate 'Women's Olympic Games' was held at Paris in 1922; just five women's athletic events were admitted in the 1928 Amsterdam Olympics) – then the fact that women figure so slightly in the history of ancient Olympia may seem less strange.

Women in Greek city-states were thoroughly domesticated: that is, they spent most of their time at home, where their main duties were raising children and making clothes. The evidence for this confined and demarcated female existence in antiquity is clear enough; even within the household, women were kept generally segregated from men. But the policies and philosophies of male-dominated Greek society did not entirely condemn women as inferior *by nature*. If women were excluded from athletics, it was not so much that they were deemed physically incapable, but rather that such activity was thought irrelevant or improper for them.

So Greek mythology spoke of a huntress, Atalanta, who could run faster than any man; and an all-female Asian tribe, the Amazons, whose fighting prowess was fearsome. In Greek history, it was Lycurgus, legendarily responsible for setting up key elements of the constitution of Sparta in archaic times, who established the extraordinary Spartan practice of allowing girls to exercise naked with boys – running, wrestling, discus-throwing, and all – with the express eugenic purpose of matching strong young men to equally strong young women (Plutarch, *Lycurgus* 14–15). It took a Roman satirist to mock the idea of women engaging in combat sports, or simply using the gymnasium (Juvenal, *Satires* 6. 246–67, 419–23); more seriously, Plato used the example of Sparta to outline a theoretical ideal of women being trained in a certain range of athletic events – though not always following the male habit of nudity (*Laws* 833c–d).

Plato's reason for female athletics is overtly stated. In case all the men of a city have to march away, the women must provide garrisons of defence. This martial justification is as we should expect from Plato and of course it is in keeping with the overall logic that so long as women were not actually involved in war, there was little cause for them to become involved in 'war minus the shooting'. Nevertheless, Olympia was not completely closed to female spectators or female participants.

We have already encountered Kyniska, the Spartan lady who was the owner-trainer of a twice-winning chariot-team at Olympia in the early fourth century BC. An inscription to be seen in the museum at Olympia (*IvO* 160) records her pride in the achievement, being then 'the only woman of all Greece' to take this crown. Pausanias also tells us of a mother, known as Kallipateira ('Of Splendid Parentage') or Pherenike ('Victory-bearer'), who brought her son to win the Olympic boys' boxing in 404 BC (5.6.7–8). Kallipateira had come to Olympia disguised as a man, because the rules forbade married women to be present; when her boy gained victory, however, she vaulted over the fence behind which all the trainers were kept, and in doing so revealed her female identity. She would have been punished by death; but, being herself the daughter and sister of Olympic champions, Kallipateira was forgiven (for more on this remarkable Rhodian family, see p. 153; the story of the disguised mother is also retailed in Philostratos, *On Gymnastics* 17 – though such repetition is no guarantee of credibility).

Pausanias does not explain why married women were excluded from the Olympic festival, though he is aware of an exception being made for the woman appointed priestess of Demeter Chamyne, Demeter 'whose bed is the Earth' – the goddess whose fertility cult at Olympia probably preceded the organized Games. To this day, the isolated marble seat reserved for this priestess may be seen on the north bank of the Stadium. (One occupant around the time of Pausanias was Regilla, wife of Herodes Atticus – who, like her husband, was a generous donor to the site.) Pausanias does tell us, though, that unmarried girls ('virgins': *parthenoi*) were permitted to watch the boys' and men's events; and that for 'maidens', too, there was a separate minor athletic festival in honour of Hera (5.16.2–8).

We do not know much about these 'Heraia' rites at Olympia – only what Pausanias tells us, and it is likely that he, as a man, was never present as a witness to them. The occasion required a newly woven robe, or *peplos*, to be offered up to Hera, presumably to adorn her temple image. The weaving of this robe was done by sixteen local married women, who also served as organizers of a series of running-races open to girls of various ages. These girls did not compete naked, but in short dresses unhitched at one shoulder (or a male-style cloak), with their hair flying loose. Apparently they ran just a one-way *stade*-race: Pausanias mentions only that the main Stadium was used, but shortened by one-sixth of its normal length – so the girls sprinted about 160 metres. The prizes were olive-leaf wreaths, with a sacrificial feast, as for the men; and the dedication of victory-images was allowed, although Pausanias does not describe any. The existence of female athletics at

Olympia was undoubtedly of prime cultic importance – a filament of tradition duly stitched into the mythology of the site. But the glory of winning at Olympia was almost wholly reserved for the men and boys.

A Note on Nudity

One reason why female spectators were barred from the main Olympic festival must have been because so many male competitors were on view without clothes. Apart from the chariot-drivers, who customarily wore a long white robe down to their ankles, the athletes at Olympia stripped for action. This is one aspect of the ancient Games that has never been revived, and it is doubtful if it even survived into the period when Greece came under Roman administration (during the second century BC). As we have seen, the Greek concept of a gymnasium literally entailed a place where nudity was routine. But the Greeks were conscious that the habit of exercising unclothed was culturally peculiar to them. And for some Greeks, at least, the gathering at Olympia was understood as a direct cause of this cultural peculiarity.

Thucydides (1.6) believed that Spartans set the example of competing unclothed and anointing themselves with oil for gymnastic exercise; he also implies that Spartan practice affected Olympia, where athletes had once been used to wearing belts across their midriffs. A more specific tradition, related not only by several ancient historians but also inscribed in a presumed epitaph (*IG* 7.52), tells us that Greek athletic nudity began at the Olympiad of 720 BC, when a sprinter called Orsippos, from Megara, won the *stade*-race – having lost his *perizoma* or loin-cloth *en route*. Evidently the loss of the loin-cloth was perceived as an advantage for velocity, because a Spartan runner called Akanthos promptly won the double-*stade* event unclad. And so, it seems, a custom was born.

Could just one episode of accidental nakedness give rise to a widespread shift in taboos or sensibilities about bodily display? To students of Greek art, the chronology is plausible enough: for it is from about 700 BC onwards that we witness, in various parts of the Greek world, the appearance of *kouros*-figures: those distinctive statues of young men in their physical prime, usually wearing nothing at all. Few of these *kouroi*, it is true, have been found in the Peloponnese: but their bold nudity at least appears to confirm that Olympia's institutional precedent was not eccentric.

That archaic Greek sculptors set about representing the poise and musculature of powerful and youthful males with increasing attention to anatomical accuracy is well known. We have already alluded to the formula, at first aristocratic and then philosophical, of *kalos kai aga-thos*, 'beautiful and good', which each nude *kouros* seems so eager to exemplify. The aesthetic force of the Classical nude resonates down the ages, and there is no need to explain it any further here. As for the erotic contingencies of nude competition, it is perhaps enough to recall that Greek athletes, especially wrestlers, customarily took the precaution of avoiding unwanted erections by tying a tight string knot around their foreskins. But how should we summarize the essential significance of nudity at the ancient Olympics?

Two historical anecdotes may tell us all we need to know. Both are connected with a Spartan – the military commander and king, Agesilaos (444–360 BC). The first story occurs in an account of a Spartan campaign against the Persians in Asia Minor, towards the end of the fifth century BC. Spartan forces commanded by Agesilaos were outnumbered, and far from home. One way by which Agesilaos bolstered their morale, we are told, was to make an exhibition of some Persian prisoners stripped bare. The sight of their soft white effete bodies heartened the Spartans. Clearly these types had not trained in the gymnasium or *palaistra*. In battle, it would be like fighting against women (Xenophon, *Hellenica* 3.4.18–19).

The second episode happens several years later, when Sparta itself is under attack from Thebes. During the defence operation, a Spartan called Isidas – 'a boy on the verge of becoming a man' – took it into his head to sally into battle stark naked (*gymnos*) and anointed with oil as if for the gymnasium. Was it the fury with which he fought – or the sheer intimidating effect of his physique as he pushed through the ranks? At any rate, Isidas caused death and mayhem among the enemy, with no harm to himself. He was subsequently disciplined for reckless fighting – but also awarded a garland for his conspicuous action (Plutarch, *Agesilaos* 34. 6–8).

The lesson of both incidents is clear. For all that nudity may be a sort of 'costume' in Greek and Roman art, and a 'habit' of Greek athletics, it is also a revelation. What you see is what you get. Sporting prowess and fighting spirit: both are made equally evident by a display of the male body without clothes.

4

SWEET VICTORY

A wreath of leaves was the simple prize to which the greatest athletes of the Classical world aspired. At Olympia, the award was woven of olive sprays. The Pythian Games at Delphi offered garlands taken from the laurel bush. The Isthmian Games called for pine; at Nemea it was wild celery or parsley.

Whatever the foliage, the Greek name for this prize is enough to suggest its symbolic importance. The victor's reward was a 'crown' (*stephanos*); figuratively, this was a regal honour. So the girls who ran in the races for Hera were crowned as if queens; so every winning male athlete at Olympia could parade himself in virtual majesty. The anticipation of modern idiom, especially in the ambience of boxing – Muhammed Ali saluted as 'King of the Ring', another fighter who styles himself 'Prince' – may make us complacent about such pretensions to royalty. But some scholars have taken it very seriously, to the extent of proposing that the primal origins of athletic contests should be located in rites of kingship or succession to a throne.

Discussion of theories about Olympic origins belongs to a subsequent chapter. But one problem with the notion that 'crowning' a Classical champion carried intimations of royalty must be immediately raised. Adornment with a chaplet or fillet (*tainia*) is often glimpsed in ancient iconography: such headpieces, usually fashioned from wool, were clearly deemed appropriate for various occasions – a funeral, a drinking party, a religious procession. And contests of all sorts, not only those of physical prowess, might offer garlands as trophies of excellence. When we speak of individuals 'resting on their laurels' we refer to the practice of decking the locks of a victorious poet or musician with Apollo's favoured bay leaves – customary not only at Delphi but also other sanctuaries where Apollo was honoured. It has been claimed that at Olympia, victorious athletes acquired semi-divine status by wearing the same olive crown as was to be seen on the statue of Zeus Olympios, created by the Athenian sculptor Pheidias in the second half of the fifth century BC. But it is likely that the Zeus of Pheidias adopted the olive crown from mortal practice. The wreath is not one of the god's usual or ubiquitous attributes.

Why a garland of olive – to be more precise, the wild olive (*kotinos*)? According to one antiquarian source,

Phlegon of Tralles, it came about as follows. For the first five Olympiads, no victory-crowns were on offer. Then an archaic king of Elis, Iphitos – whom Pausanias salutes as one who did much to formalize the Games – consulted the Delphic Oracle on the question of awarding crowns. The oracular reply was typically peculiar and specific. It told Iphitos not to use 'the produce of the sheep' (or, in ambivalent Greek, 'the fruit of the apple') for a garland, but rather to seek out an undomesticated olive tree '*now wrapped in the spider's fine net*'. Iphitos found such a cob-webbed olive in the Altis of Olympia, and put a wall around it. The first athlete to win a crown fashioned from this tree was one Daikles, a sprinter from Messene.

At festivals apart from the four 'Sacred and Crown Games', prizes for victory might include substantial quantities of olive oil. At the Panathenaic gathering, for instance, victors in various age categories might expect to receive many large jars (*amphorae*) of oil, which had a considerable cash value. The average 'Panathenaic amphora' had a capacity of 38–39 litres; an incomplete Athenian inscription from *c.*370 BC suggests that something like 80 to 120 jars of oil were awarded to the winner of the men's *stadion*-race, with 60 for the corresponding youths' event (12 jars for second place); while for the two-horse chariot contest it was a total of 140 jars (and 40 for second place). The recipient of 120 jars (over 4,500 litres of oil) can be estimated as having been rewarded, in today's values, to the tune of some £50,000 ($75,000).

The choice of olive leaves for the crown at Olympia may have carried some economic associations of the olive as a crop. We might also recall that every athlete valued olive oil in daily training as a lubricant and moisturizer. But ultimately there is no need to search for any precise reason for the olive as symbolic greenery. More important is to understand the potency of the symbol. In the early sixth century BC it seems that the Athenian lawgiver Solon attempted to quantify (or limit) what an Olympic victory was worth: allegedly he offered any Athenian successful at the Olympic Games the sum of 500 drachmas – a generous bounty (and the prime prestige of Olympia is already evident from the Solonian recompense for winning at the Isthmian Games – 100 drachmas). As we shall see, victory at Olympia could entail further handsome economic benefits for an athlete and his family. But our first task is to comprehend the extraordinary *kudos*, or 'glory', that came with Olympia's 'fair-crowning olive', *kotinos kallistephanos*. We should remain cautious about foisting upon antiquity the modern ideal of amateurism. All the same, it has to be admitted that this prize defies measurement in material terms.

A single aside from Greek history shows how self-conscious the Greeks could be with regard to their non-materialistic motivation for sport. The Olympic gathering was observed even during the invasion of Greece by Xerxes in 480 BC: Herodotus (8.26) reports the consternation of a Persian officer on learning that the Greeks at Olympia were competing not 'for the sake of riches' but rather 'for renown'. This chapter explores the shaping and extent of such a culture of repute.

The Olympic Victory Ceremony

In ancient athletics, as intimated earlier, it was possible – especially in the combat events – to triumph without a contest, as a 'by-sitter' (*ephedros*). But however victory was gained at Olympia, no athlete could count himself the winner until it was officially announced by a herald at the site. The broadcast message was direct enough, naming the successful athlete as 'best among the Greeks': this public 'proclamation of the crown' probably happened soon after the event, and doubtless caused immediate celebrations in the victor's camp, with the athlete collecting palm leaves and accolades. Formal 'binding of the crown' seems not to have taken place until the penultimate or final day of proceedings: whether a final prize ceremony occurred at all is queried by some scholars. There is, however, anecdoctal evidence that in the meantime some victors, most likely the afflu-ent types triumphant in the Hippodrome, organized private parties for their supporters. In the case of the incontinently ambitious Alcibiades, this was a lavish banquet, setting up a huge dais and roasting enough oxen to feed everyone at the festival. And Empedocles from Akragas (Agrigento), winning a horse-race at the 71st Olympiad of 496 BC, did not let his vegetarian principles spoil the occasion: he confected a cake in the shape of an ox, expensively spiced with frankincense and myrrh (Athenaeus 3e).

The parade of victors on the fifth or sixth day was semi-riotous – the sort of ecstatic carousel the Greeks called a *komos*. Already decked with woollen headbands – but not yet the olive crown – the victors made their way towards the Temple of Zeus. They were showered with flowers, fruit, and twigs – a 'greenery-pelting' (*phyllobolia*) which may be imagined as an organic precedent for the tribute of confetti or ticker-tape. A hymn was sung – a chorus attributed to the seventh-century BC poet Archilochos, seemingly in honour of Herakles (only dubious snatches survive: Fr. 324 West) – as the procession made its way to the Temple and Altar of Zeus. Then, in the presence of the image of Zeus Olympios, the crown of olive leaves was bestowed. The colossal ivory and gold statue of Zeus erected by Pheidias at Olympia *c.*435 BC was explicitly *Nikephoros*, 'Victory-bearing': that is, holding in one outstretched hand a figure of Victory (*Nike*), conventionally imagined as a winged female by Greek artists since the seventh century BC (**Fig. 29**). This was surely the most solemn part of the proceedings, and a sincerely religious moment. As we shall see, victory hymns composed for the Crown Games emphasized that for all an athlete's prowess and efforts, winning can happen only as an act of divine grace and favour.

Sacrifices at the Altar ensued. Over centuries of use, the Altar grew to be a conspicuous mound, built up by

29. Reconstruction, by Sian Frances, of the Olympic Zeus originally by Pheidias, *c.*435 BC. Estimated height of the statue around 14 m.

deposits of bone and ash left by offerings to Zeus: the thunderous god who at Olympia and his other leading sanctuaries was *hekatombaios* – deserving of a hundred oxen. In keeping with usual Greek tradition, the deity received parcels of bone, fat, and offal. The prime meat went to feed the mortal participants, who completed their victory ovations, and the entire Olympic festival, with a banquet in the Prytaneion, or official hall, located in the northwest corner of the Altis.

So much for the occasion of victory at Olympia itself. The rites of triumph, however, were far from over.

Naturally there were further celebrations when the victor returned home. The welcome reserved for those coming back with an Olympic crown could be spectacular, especially in the Greek colonies of the western Mediterranean. When a runner called Exainetos won his second successive victory in the *stadion*-sprint at the 92nd Olympiad of 412 BC, his native city of Akragas in Sicily greeted him with an escort of 300 chariots pulled by white horses, and a section of the city walls was knocked down for the hero's entrance. It was a symbolic breach of defences: what did the city need of walls, when it had bastions of young men like Exainetos?

How often this rite of civic reception was enacted is doubtful, though writers in Roman times considered it a custom of the Crown Games (for example, Plutarch, *Sympotic Questions* 2.5.2); and festivals that granted the privilege of bringing in the crowned victor triumphally by chariot were distinguished as 'iselastic' (*eiselastikos*: after the verb *eiselaunein*, 'to drive in'). The emperor Nero of course made sure the pageantry was fully exploited when he arrived in Italy after truly incredible successes at Olympia and Delphi in AD 66–7 – bringing home no fewer than 1,808 first-place prizes (as alleged by Dio Cassius 63.21). But evidence is also widespread for the generally unstinting treatment of victorious Olympic athletes in cities around the Classical world. Athens was not exceptional in granting, beyond a substantial cash reward, various other honours and privileges: for example, a lifetime's right to take meals at public expense (in the city's Prytaneion); front-row seats at the theatre; and tax-exemptions. No wonder that by the time of Socrates and Plato, the blessed or 'feted' existence of the Olympic victor was proverbial (*Republic* 465de). The material benefits of success might also extend to the victor's family and descendants.

But how were the moments or even the lifespans of glory to be sustained unto posterity? Because races were not timed, and the distances of jumps and throws rarely measured in absolute terms, the keeping of 'Olympic records', in our modern understanding of the term, was not important in antiquity. There is some archaeological and anecdotal evidence for the display of inscriptions giving names of victors at Olympia and Elis – or, in the case of individual winners, at prominent sites (such as gymnasia or temples) in the athlete's home town. However, no fixed roll-call of victory existed before *c.*400 BC, when the Elean Sophist Hippias (whose intellectual personality is colourfully sketched in two of Plato's dialogues) set about compiling or concocting a list of winners from the first Olympiad (776 BC) onwards. We do not know what sources were available to Hippias for this 'Olympic Victory Register', though it has long been known, thanks to its preservation in the *Chronicles* of the fourth-century Christian bishop Eusebius (giving a 'timeline' from Olympiads 1 to 249); and its 'canonical' status in antiquity confirmed by the finding and publication (in 1899) of a papyrus scrap from Oxyrhynchus in Egypt. As its excavators noted, Oxyrhynchus was 'a somewhat remote and unimportant centre of Hellenic culture'. Yet even here, around the mid-third century AD, some scribe or schoolchild appears to have copied down excerpts from a standardized record of Olympic victors, naming winners in thirteen events for Olympiads 480–468 and 456–448.

The countdown of Classical 'history' marked at each four-yearly interval since the first Olympiad – which of course only became '776 Before Christ' according to Eusebius and other Christian authorities – was already habitual by the third century BC, when it was used by Eratosthenes, the polymath scholar in charge of the library at Alexandria. Effectively, Hippias had seasoned a chronological system with winners' names, plus their events and place of provenance. The athlete triumphant in the single *stade*-race was customarily honoured as eponymous to the entire meeting. Yet this 'official' honouring of Olympic victory was hardly significant when compared with two further modes of commemoration – the victory ode and the victory statue.

Commemorating Victory

I: EPINIKIAN POEMS

'Epinikian poetry' is the categorical term of reference for the Greek victory ode, and we might as well avail ourselves of the term 'epinikian statuary' for its equivalent in sculpture, given that two media were essentially similar (if not rivals) in commission and intent. Significantly, both epinikian poetry and epinikian statuary have – and *had*, for the ancients – a particular period of their own flourishing and excellence, broadly centred in the fifth century BC. Such 'Classic' status for the poets and sculptors concerned partly reflects social and political changes at Olympia and the other Crown Games, which we shall address in the next chapter. But since poetry was always considered the superior mode of expression in Classical hierarchies of the arts, it is with the verse that we should begin.

> You must be an athlete – since nothing renders a man more renowned in his own lifetime than what he can do with his hands and his feet.

These are the words with which Laodamas, a prince of the Phaeacians, invites Homer's wandering hero Odysseus to join in some local games (*Odyssey* 8. 146–8). Odysseus, wearied by his efforts to get home after serving at Troy, at first declines the invitation. Then one Phaeacian youth taunts him, scorning this reluctance to compete as a sign that Odysseus is a mere sea-faring trader, more interested in pursuing profit than sport. Odysseus gives the best heroic riposte. Without even bothering to shrug off his cloak, he strides over to the discus-throwing area, and picks up a discus that is much bigger and heavier than the local competitors have dared to use. He takes one swing and launches the weight on its way. It hums through the air – and lands way beyond the marks made by everyone else. Odysseus turns and asks if there is anything else they want to try him at – boxing, wrestling, javelin, archery, running? But he has made his point. The company meekly adjourns for drinking and songs.

Homer was not an epinikian bard; the world he described predates the Panhellenic festivals. But the glee with which this episode is told, and the very sentiment voiced by Laodamas, show Homer as the prototypical mentor of the epinikian mode. Gaining fame is the compulsive motive for taking part in sport. Fame is the victor's greatest reward. And to ensure that he receives it, the poet must assist.

The formal 'victory hymn', or *epinikion melos*, may have its origins in the output of the abrasive and sensuous seventh-century lyric poet Archilochos, who (as mentioned above) appears to have composed the customary chorus for the crowning procession in Olympia's Altis. It is a moot point whether poets regularly attended the Olympic festival in order to compose and deliver *epinikia* on the occasion of the olive-wreath ceremony:

while it is hard to believe that the masters of this genre never witnessed the athletic triumphs they were called upon to celebrate, it is also demonstrable that many surviving examples were intended for performance at the subsequent reception of the victor by his native or sponsoring city-state. In any case, the first acknowledged master of the epinikian form was Simonides of Keos, *c*.556–468 BC, who seems to have been proud to make the composition of such lyrics a full-time, well-paid *métier*. His epinikian output, much respected in antiquity, survives only in fragments and citations. It is clear enough, however, that Simonides set the precedent for political promiscuity in the epinikian mode: that is to say, he would write as glowingly in honour of a tyrant or the citizen-athlete of a democratic *polis*. Notoriously, he did not disdain to apostrophize a team of hard-flogged mules as '*daughters of storm-footed steeds!*' – so long as a good fee was offered.

Simonides had a nephew, Bacchylides, who also specialized in the genre. Ibycus, a distinguished sixth-century lyricist from the western Greek colony of Rhegium (Reggio), occasionally turned his skills to epinikian too. But one name above all is associated with this form of composition: Pindar (518–438 BC).

Pindar's origins were in Boeotia, but, like Simonides, he travelled wherever patronage beckoned. His victory-odes have survived relatively intact, and attest the demand for his services not only at Olympia but also at the Isthmian, Nemean, and Pythian Games. Evidently his work was valued highly during his lifetime (and the epinikian poets were, of course, competing among themselves as literary *virtuosi* when they sang of athletic champions); and Pindar's output has not really fallen out of favour with readers and commentators ever since.

The principles of what Pindar was aiming to achieve with each of his epinikian odes have been adroitly summarized (by Charles Segal) as a simple quartet. First, the poetry salutes the achievement of an individual victor. Second – often drawing on the pedigree of myth – it relates the immediate victory to the athlete's nurturing within a particular family group and city-state. Third, it emphasizes the effort and exertion demanded of athletic victory, pledging a hope for continued success in the future. And fourth, as Segal outlines, Pindaric epinikian 'reincorporates the victor into the community and into the values of the community': a necessary move, since triumph carries the risk of envy (*phthonos*) from gods and fellow mortals, and the danger of over-weening pride (*hubris*) from the athlete.

The language used by Pindar is, at one level, very simple and direct. In the words of one of the poet's most eloquent modern expositors, Basil Gildersleeve, Pindar 'drains dry the Greek vocabulary of words for light and bright, shine and shimmer, glitter and glister, ray and radiance, flame and flare and flash, gleam and glow, burn and blaze'. In fact Greek epinikian verse in general is permeated with the quality of *aglaia*: a term of poetic approval encompassing whatever is splendid, adorning, and eye-catching, whether the pearly-glints of an oyster shell or a boxer dressed in sweat.

Given this straightforwardness of poetic intent and tone, it might be imagined that Pindar's victory-songs are easy to comprehend and translate. On the contrary: they are sturdily resistant both to full understanding and effective translation. So it is with due sense of lacklustre inadequacy that the following rendition of Pindar's Eighth Olympian Ode is offered here.

The occasion is the victory of Alkimedon of Aegina in the boys' wrestling at the 80th Olympiad of 460 BC. It is with the site and sanctuary of Olympia that the poet begins:

> Mother of goldcrowned games, Olympia,
> sovereign of truths; where prophet-priests
> seek from sacrifice and flames to know
> what plans are nursed by thunderburdened Zeus
> for men whose heart's desire
> yearns for a great renown –
> and respite from their toil.
>
> For mortal prayers bring on reward for piety.
> So, from Pisa's leafy precincts by the Alpheios
> welcome now this garlandwearing band!
> Glory is always great
> for whoever takes that shimmering prize.
> To one man or another
> good things are bestowed.
> There are many routes to happiness
> with the gods.

Destiny, Timosthenes, made you and your kin
the darlings of Zeus.
You won your fame at Nemea.
Now for Alkimedon: blessed with victory
at Olympia, by the slopes of Kronos.
On first sight he was splendid; sure
he proved his beauty in the test.
Triumphant from each bout
he put his homeland on the herald's lips –
'Aegina of the long oars!'
where saviour-goddess Themis
enthroned with all-fathering Zeus
is honoured more devoutly than

by any men elsewhere. For when matters of
    importance
hang much in the balance
it's a heavy wrestle for rightminded men
to make decisions well.
But by order of the gods
so too this seabound place
has risen as a divine pillar
for pilgrims from afar.
And may time to come
not cease to keep it that way.

Pindar's hymn to young Alkimedon is arranged in
a 'triadic' sequence of stanzas designed to assist and
direct the rhythms of a choral performance. Did such
a performance take place at Olympia, during victory
celebrations at the site, or back on Alkimedon's home
island of Aegina? Hints in the text are ambivalent, and
perhaps intentionally so, allowing the piece to be

delivered at either location (or indeed both). In any case, Pindar begins by saluting Olympia as site of the victory; and he loses no time in stressing the sacrosanct context in which victory was gained. The divination process (see p. 175) is immediately evoked; and a wide audience assumed of those coming to the sanctuary with hopes of renown (*aretê*) or relief from exertion (*mochthos*). It is an epinikian commonplace that *aretê* cannot come without heavy expenditure of *mochthos*; but even so, divine favour is the absolute condition.

Elsewhere (*Pythian* 8.96) Pindar will speak of victory as a 'god-given radiance'. Here we are soon made aware that such heavenly favour is not confined to an individual victor, but also extends to his close family and descendants. Pindar's first address is to Timosthenes, probably a brother of Alkimedon, who has been successful at the Nemean Games. Describing Alkimedon himself, the poet is content to say merely that he was 'beautiful' (*kalos*) of aspect – with the crucial rider, 'and he confirmed his beauty on the field', relying upon an audience understanding not only of beauty equated with goodness, but also beauty defined by athletic supremacy. (And that, as we saw in Chapter 2, was an expectation firmly promoted by sculptors of the period.)

The poet proceeds to sing of the victor's provenance:

Aegina: held on behalf of the Dorian race
since the days of Aiakos.
He it was whom Leto's boy [Apollo]
with Poseidon of boundless domain

intent on ringing Ilium
with diadem of walls
made partner in the work;
since fate called for towers
that in the midst of war
and terrorspewing strife
should sigh with smoke beyond control.

Bluegreen dragons – the bulwark just built –
came clawing up the heights. Three of them there
  were:
two dropped down, dizzy and dead;
the third reached the top with a snarl.
Apollo saw immediately what this dire omen meant.
'There goes Pergamos, hero [Aiakos] –
taken where you laboured with your hands.
So it is revealed to me
in a vision from Zeus himself –
Zeus the thunderloosing son of Kronos.
And not without your sons. A first generation,
then a third, will bring the city down.' So
the god relayed his message, and took himself
fullspeed to Xanthos; onward to the Amazons
with their fine cavalry, on further
to the Danube's stream.
Meanwhile the tridentshaker
powered his fast chariot
towards seabordered Isthmus:
bearing Aiakos homeward
by horses of gold –

so returning to preside on Corinthian shores
at festivals famed abroad.
Well – there is no such thing as a pleasure to all men.

If I pace ahead with my song
and tell of glory due to Melesias
prizewinner amid the beardless young
let me not be struck by envy's sharp stone.
I could proclaim of his own youthful triumph
at Nemea; not to mention, later on,
his victory among fighting men
in the pankration. To teach is easy enough
when one knows what it takes; but hopeless
without apprenticeship. Inexpertise
blows bubble-advice. Melesias taught above all
on the base of his own great deeds;
showing an athlete how to prepare
to gain the ultimate prize
at one of the Sacred Games. So today
Melesias has his due. It's Alkimedon –
taking a thirtieth win.

By heavensent good grace? Yes – but a show of
    strength no less,
loading the limbs of four other lads
with the loser's hateful return (the jeering voices,
the furtive back-alleys)
while giving his father's father
the will to combat with old age.
For Hades gets forgotten
In the family's success.
But let us now call from memory's store
and refresh the flowers of victory
in Blepsiad hands. This is their sixth crown
from garlandgiving games. So the dead, too,
will savour offerings properly made.
No dust shall obscure
the great glory accrued by such kin.

So when tidings arrive from the angel of Fame –
Hermes' daughter she is –
Iphion shall tell Kallimachos his brother
what radiant honour at Olympia
has come to the clan from Zeus.
May the god pile good things upon good things
diverting all bitter distress.
And I pray this: that with the grant of a well-earned
    reward
there shall be no disputes in its share.
Let life go unharmed, let the family bloom –
them and their city as well.

What Alkimedon has gained in person by winning the boys' wrestling at Olympia is left almost entirely implicit in this ode. Pindar is more eager to pursue the reflected glory. So Alkimedon's birthplace, Aegina, is cited as a major beneficiary of the win. To judge from the number of odes he composed for local athletes, Pindar enjoyed particular favour among the Aeginetan gentry. Here the island is implicitly likened to Olympia as a place of time-honoured sanctity, where in addition to Zeus, the justice-goddess Themis enjoys particular veneration. Themis deserves worship, Pindar declares, because taking good judgements is 'hard wrestling' (*dyspalês*: an oblique reference to the event in which Alkimedon won his crown). A lesson in local mythography ensues – with political undertones.

Aiakos was the hero-founder of Aegina as a state. His chronological location as a demigod (the offspring of Zeus and a nymph called Aegina) is indicated by the story Pindar narrates of how Aiakos was recruited by Apollo and Poseidon to assist in constructing the walls of Troy (referred to as either 'Ilium' or 'Pergamos' in the ode); then to learn, by Apollo's foresight, of how his own legendary descendants would be involved in destroying those very same fortifications. So, of the three dragons envisaged attacking the towers Aiakos has helped to build, seemingly the two who fall back defeated are the grandsons of Aiakos, Achilles, and Ajax. Vengeful triumph is reserved for Neoptolemos, the son of Achilles (therefore great-grandson of Aiakos).

Without scrutinizing Pindar's terse (and problematic) presentation of this story, we may wonder what possible bearing it has upon the Olympic success of Alkimedon. Very little, on the face of it. But when we learn that this ode was composed at a time of pained historical uncertainty for Aegina, Pindar's motives become more clear. Aegina had been more or less at war with Athens since 506 BC. In 459, a year after Alkimedon's victory at Olympia, there was a resumption of hostilities, which would end two years later in the island's submission to Athenian sea-power. So Pindar's story of a city built and a city ruined adds a timely tincture of elegiac bitterness to his song of athletic success.

It may then have been a matter of diplomatic delicacy that Alkimedon's trainer, Melesias, was an Athenian. If so, Pindar includes him for praise all the same. Mentioned in other epinikian odes, Melesias evidently ran a successful 'stable' of young athletes, with Alkimedon raising his tally of proprietorial victories to thirty. But his semi-paternal role as trainer, or *aleiptês*, is all the more significant here, since it appears that Alkimedon was an orphan. So news of the boy's victory must be conducted to his father (and uncle) in the Underworld, via Hermes and daughter.

How many of Alkimedon's family, the Aeginetan *genos* collectively known as the Blepsiadai (after an ancestor called Blepsias), were around to hear this ode, we cannot say. It seems a grandfather was alive to take cheer from it all (and again Alkimedon's event provides the metaphor for a 'wrestling-against', or *antipalos*, to geriatric distress). Certainly, however, there was little in Pindar's hymn of praise to Alkimedon that would have caused the boy himself to blush. Beyond the single allusion to his good looks, there is no descriptive detail about how his victory was gained – only the mention that in the course of four bouts Alkimedon avoided the humiliating experience of losing, 'shifting' that shame onto his opponents. Other epinikian poets – notably Bacchylides – were more enthusiastic in evoking the contest as such. Pindar is more concerned with not only the consequences of athletic victory, but also its fertilization in immediate and mythical ancestry, cult observance, careful training – and sheer hard labour.

When Alcibiades won at Olympia, the Athenian dramatist and poet Euripides composed a brief epinikian that hailed his victory (accurately enough) as *aponêtos* – 'effortless'. Pindar would never have eulogized success in that way. For Pindar, no crown could be gained without 'toil' (*ponos*; likewise *mochthos*, and *kamatos*). If athletic endeavour offered mortals the opportunity to become heroes, then athletes, like heroes, must be subject to fearsome or fatally dangerous ordeals. Victory brought exquisite happiness – or at least as much happiness as anyone on earth could hope for; and that state of being was all the more blissful for being reached by suffering and risk.

To those who take up the challenge of athletic excellence, Pindar pledges his epinikian hymns as a sweetly distilled *nektar* of reward (in the opening address of *Olympian* 7). In advertising his own lyric gifts, however, the poet is not only in competition with other poets. The epinikian poets liked to think that their commemorations of success were uniquely portable from one place to another and uniquely durable over time. But in both these respects, they faced serious rivalry from artists in other media – in particular from sculptors.

II: EPINIKIAN STATUES

Some Olympic victors were evidently commemorated in pictures. For his sweeping triumph in the chariot-race, Alcibiades was represented as being crowned by a female personification of Olympia – the work of a painter called Aglaophon (Athenaeus 534d). Another athlete was depicted – by Eupompos of Sikyon – in the act of holding a victory palm (Pliny, *Natural History* 35.36). The range of such two-dimensional athletic art is partially reflected in the many graphic sporting vignettes that have survived on Greek painted pottery. Also from further afield: one Etruscan tomb, coincidentally brought to light around the time of the 1960 Rome Olympics, shows large-scale images of chariot-racing, running, jumping, and discus-throwing (Fig. 30). However, no works by the 'great masters' of Classical Greek painting have survived. So when we come to assess the commemoration of Olympic victory in figurative art, the focus is inevitably upon statues.

As much epinikian poetry remains in fragments, so epinikian statuary has suffered the plight of transience.

30. Detail of the 'Tomb of the Olympic Games' at Tarquinia, *c*.500 BC: a pair of not-quite naked runners.

Of all the excavated finds from Olympia, no relics are more pathetic than the scatter of numerous metallic minor body parts – lips, eyelashes, ears, genitalia – that are the only remnants of what was once a huge population of hollow bronze statues raised to champion athletes. Broken up to be melted down, these figures displayed one feature bound to invite Christian or Vandal attack in late antiquity – their shameless nudity. But whether smashed *in situ*, or else lost centuries after being removed from the sanctuary by Roman collectors, the Olympic victor statues have not entirely surrendered to oblivion. Many were seen and patiently recorded by Pausanias when he made his visit to Olympia in the mid-second century AD. Many of the inscribed bases upon which the statues once stood have now been excavated. And precisely because the Romans valued them as *objets d'art*, some of these statues, and many others like them, have survived in marble copies or adaptations. So, as a type of Classical sculpture, the image of the crowned athlete has lasted to posterity; and, as a type, has served as one of the most forceful icons of Classical identity in Western culture (Fig. 31).

Pindar (*Nemean* 5.49) envisaged a trainer in the gymnasium as builder or 'joiner' (*tektôn*) of athletes. The 'tectonics' of athletic eminence as crafted in gymnasium and *palaistra* we have already explored (see p. 58). Myron, Polykleitos, and other sculptors of fifth-century BC Greece collaborated and competed in creating a stereotype of the winning body: ultimately a muscular

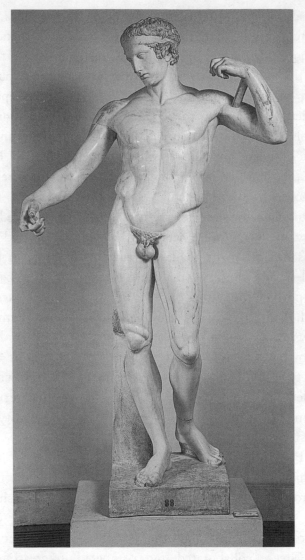

31. Diadumenos or 'crowned athlete': marble copy after a bronze original by Polykleitos.

template that would incorporate not only the mingled virtuous signals of 'beautiful goodness' – heroic stature, military readiness, and athletic triumph – but also carry the imprint of cosmic mathematical harmony. So the physique of an Olympic victor, for all its bulk and heft, came nevertheless to represent a sort of transcendental grace: a symmetry of form first constructed by hard training, then refined by the sculptors and their geometric calculations before being cast in bronze.

The process of hollow bronze casting by the 'lost wax' technique is too complex to describe here. It is sufficient to understand that working in thin-walled bronze favoured the making of life-size or larger-scale statues in action poses, with various possibilities for marking subtle details such as hair, sinews, and veins. A saying attributed to Polykleitos, the most influential of fifth-century epinikian sculptors, goes: *The work is hardest when the clay is on the nail*. This probably alludes to the essential preliminary process of making (to scale) a clay figure from which the cast is to be taken, and indicates the fastidious delicacy of a sculptor shaping final features with pinpoint or fingernail. An Athenian vase shows us the later stage of assembling and soldering together various cast body parts (**Fig. 32**). (By nice coincidence, the scraping tool used for smoothing down the bronze surface is almost identical to the strigil used by athletes after workouts.)

The bronze-casting process favoured the making of a series of similar figures. The Riace Bronzes, for example,

32. Making bronze statues: detail of an Athenian red-figure cup by the so-called 'Foundry Painter', c.480 BC. The 'decapitated' figure on the right will probably be the image of a wrestler about to engage.

were demonstrably cast from more or less the same basic prototype (see Fig. 14). This suited the tendency, at Olympia, for the statues of victors to be clustered according to athletic speciality, *polis* origins, or family groups. It is clear from the way in which Pausanias records his tour of statuary in the Altis that such themed clusters could be envisaged like factions, taking up their positions around the Temple of Zeus, each with a claim on divine favour. The first group encountered by Pausanias, for example, was made up of several victors united by the fact that they were all of Spartan origin, and all triumphant in equestrian disciplines (6. 1.6–2.1).

Permission to erect statues came from the Council-House of the Elean administrators at Olympia. But commemorations of victory did not have to be immediate; monuments could be erected many years in retrospect, making it all the more feasible for an athletically successful family to celebrate its lineage. So, for example, Pausanias encountered an *ex voto* assemblage at Olympia that was a formidable line-up of hefty fighters, the 'Diagorids' from Ialysos on Rhodes (6.7.1–2). Chronologically the founder of this lineage was Diagoras: standing at a reported six feet and six inches tall, he was not only winner of the men's boxing in 464 BC, but also a 'circuit-winner' – that is, he collected the crown for boxing also at the Pythian, Isthmian, and Nemean Games. Pindar's *Olympian* 7 was devoted to Diagoras, but even Pindar could hardly have predicted the run of subsequent triumphs. The oldest son of Diagoras was

Damagetos, winner of the *pankration* at Olympia in both 452 and 448 BC. A second son, Akousilaos, won the Olympic boxing in 448; and a third son, Dorieus, was circuit-winner no fewer than three times between 432 and 424. Then, it seems, a daughter of Diagoras also gave rise to further champions: Eukles, victor in the men's boxing at the 94th Olympiad of 404 BC; and Peisirhodos, victor in the boys' boxing at the same meeting. From two excavated bases we discover that the sculptor of the figure of Diagoras was Kallikles of Megara, while that of Eukles was done by Naukydes of Argos, so the statues were probably commissioned on separate occasions: first Diagoras and his sons, perhaps, then his two grandsons. The group was evidently moved around in antiquity, and Diagoras as patriarch dominated it by his physical presence (though the family came to grief politically, Diagoras enjoyed lasting heroization as a 'son of Herakles', with Pindar's ode to him inscribed on a gold plaque and displayed in the Temple of Athena at Lindos on Rhodes). Nonetheless, the Diagorid group must have been physiognomically coherent – and very much occupying its own collective space amid the forest of statues within the Altis.

We have alluded to the capacity for the hollow bronze-casting process to capture action poses. Myron, author of the original 'Discobolos' (see Fig. 18), was famed for an image which remains difficult to visualize – a statue celebrating a runner called Ladas, apparently caught in full flight, with every muscle straining in the effort to be first. Perhaps this was the same Ladas whose grave in Laconia was noted by Pausanias (3.21.1) with the supposition that the effort proved fatal; in any case, we have only a later poetic salutation by which to assess the statue's breathtaking impact.

> Soon this bronze will leap to take the crown, escape its pedestal. Look how art goes faster than the wind!
>
> (*Greek Anthology* 16.54)

The hope of sculptors being able to capture a moment of total kinetic exertion was optimistic (most modern sports photographers prefer to fix speed as a shutter-blur); more readily imaginable than a sprinter, perhaps, is the boxer whose statue-base declares:

> Just so, upright by the Alpheios, this Pelasgian boxer once showed with his hands the precepts of Polydeukes, and was heralded as victor. So, father Zeus, renew Arcadia's delightful glory [*kleos*], and honour Philippos who in quick fisticuffs here laid low four island boys.
>
> (*IvO* 174)

Inscribed on a bronze plaque, this declaration of distilled praise is not entirely clear in its implications for the pose of its honorand, Philippos (a young victor at Olympia *c.*300 BC). Polydeukes is Pollux, one of the two Dioskouroi, who mythically won the first boxing match at Olympia, in the proto-Games established by Herakles (see Pausanias 5.8.4; though Pindar *Olympian* 10.67 tells a different tale). The 'precepts' (*nomoi*) of Polydeukes may be connected with good pugilistic form, or simply some gesture of self-acclaim. Either way, the statue's achievement was to 'freeze' a superb moment. So bronze redeemed the transience of a 'crowning glory' and a crown made only of leaves (**Fig. 33**).

The marble bases or platforms on which these victory statues stood tended to be lowly in height, emphasizing the physical presence of the bronze figure on top, but not at all discreet about their inscribed purpose. Engraved epigrams echoed to posterity the heraldic announcements of victory; and left viewers in no doubt as to how the statues above were to be regarded. The following lines, attributed to Simonides, accompanied a statue of one Theognetos, winner of the boys' wrestling at Olympia in 476 BC:

> Know what you see when you gaze upon this: it is Theognetos, boy-champion of Olympia, who skilfully steered his course to victory in the wrestling-ring. Most beautiful to behold, most formidable to challenge, here is a youth who crowned the city of his good forefathers.
>
> (*Greek Anthology* 16.2)

The question of how far these victory statues were recognizable portraits of the athletes they commemorated is impossible to resolve. (Pliny, in his *Natural History* 34.16, suggests that a three-times Olympic victor was

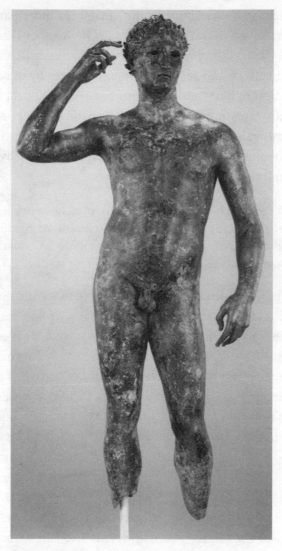

33. Bronze statue of an athlete crowning himself, late fourth
century BC. Height 151.5 cm. Traces of the wreath around this
athlete's head indicate olive leaves, therefore an Olympic
significance.

entitled to an especially 'iconic' image – a more particular sort of physical simulacrum.) The 'captions' of the statue-bases, however, were always important aids to identification; and served to engage passers-by in several ways. Some, like the lines from Simonides above, begin with an arresting imperative command. Others reflect the ambivalence of Greek reading habits at the time – silently or aloud. So an inscription recorded at Olympia by Pausanias (6.3.14) runs as follows:

> In the much-frequented sanctuary of heavenruling Zeus I stand, dedicated by the citizens of Samos. Lysander, you have won undying glory for Aristokritos and your homeland: well-known for courage.

Here, the abrupt switch from first- to second-person verbal address halfway through the inscription requires its reader to begin by reproducing, as it were, the voice of the statue – standing for the Spartan commander Lysander – and then to vocalize a viewer's share of praising the same statue. In this case (as Pausanias notes) the dedication of Lysander's image was a piece of political opportunism, but its terminology of 'undying glory' and 'courage', along with the pious inclusion of Lysander's father Aristokritos, is entirely characteristic of epinikian statue-bases. And we should not be surprised by the notion of a sculpted figure possessing a voice. The sanctuaries of the Classical world were densely crowded with statues that stood not just as 'doubles' of the deities and mortals they represented, but whose existence was

widely perceived as vivid and independent. To understand the nature of that perception, we need to investi-
gate further the formal development of 'naturalistic'
style in epinikian commissions of the fifth century BC.

Pausanias does not transcribe the legend carved on
the base of the statue of Kyniskos, victor in the boys'
boxing at the Olympiad of 460 BC. He simply notes
(6.4.11) that it was made by Polykleitos. The statue is
gone; but the base has been excavated (*IvO* 149). In
content, the inscription is not especially original –
merely declaring that the statue was set up by the boxer
Kyniskos, son of Kyniskos, from the 'well-reputed' city
of Mantinea. What is more interesting is the way in
which this information is released as a spiral around the
base, leading the viewer around the statue in a circuit of
appreciative assessment. From front, sides, and rear, the
fine points of this young champion's winning form are
equally to be judged. No less important is the demand
made upon the viewer to inspect this as a work of art. As
far as we can judge from pieces probably derived from
this statue (see Fig. 31), the posture of the victorious
Kyniskos was not overtly proud. There is no raised fist of
triumph, not even a smile – rather, as the boy crowns
himself, a downcast expression of almost melancholic
modesty, verging on shame. As Pindar overlooked young
Alkimedon in his hymn of praise, so Polykleitos does not
invest his epinikian statue of Kyniskos with any measure
of boastful ecstasy. The decorum of the sculptor's art
demanded otherwise.

In fact epinikian statuary at Olympia did not materialize as a genre until the fifth century BC, with one of the earliest examples reflected in copies of a 'Discobolos' in the so-called 'Severe Style' of Greek sculpture (**Fig. 34**). The tradition of dedicating small-scale solid bronzes at the site was much older (see p. 233), and during the sixth century we find individual athletes dedicating certain relevant sporting objects *ex voto* – such as the jumping-weights or *diskoi* they had used in competition. One archaic marble figure of the *kouros* type (of a young man in a standing pose), made *c.*570 BC and found at Phigaleia in Arcadia, has been suggested as an early victor-statue (of the doomed pankratiast Arrhachion: see Pausanias 8.40.1), though a smaller hollow-bronze *kouros* recovered from Olympia remains an exceptional piece for the period. The earliest statues of victors recorded by Pausanias (6.18.7) in his tour of the Altis are those of Praxidamas, a boxer from Aegina triumphant in the Olympiad of 544 BC, and the pankratiast Rhexibios, from 536 BC.

No trace of either statue has been found. Frustratingly, too, we have no material evidence of the statue raised in the late sixth century BC to Milo of Croton, which is celebrated in a later poetic epigram as '*The handsome statue of handsome Milo, who in Pisa's precincts was victorious seven times, and not once felled to his knees*' (*Greek Anthology* 16.24). Evidently Milo was shown standing on a circular basis that looked like a *diskos*, and with one hand extended holding a pomegranate.

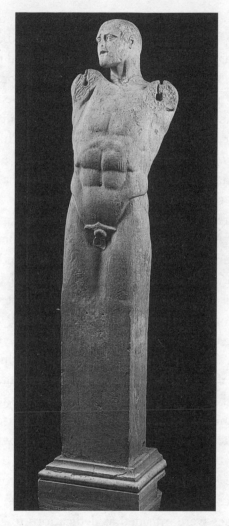

34. Discobolos: marble copy after a Greek bronze original *c.*470–
460 BC. Formerly in the Ludovisi Collection, this 'hip-herm' or
semi-full-length figure was probably created in the second
century BC to decorate a Roman garden.

Pausanias (6.14.6) explains this pose with anecdotes about how Milo would stand on a discus and defy anyone to budge him; or take a pomegranate and challenge all comers to prise it from his grip. Much more likely is that the athlete was represented in the votive stance of offering the fruit to Hera – a likelihood half-understood by another late witness of the statue (see Philostratos, *Life of Apollonius* 4.28).

Epinikian statuary, then, was created as a genre in the fifth century BC by bronze-working specialists trained predominantly in the north Peloponnesian centres of Argos and Sikyon, with some influence also from Athens and Aegina. As a trade it tended to be hereditary, and dominated by a few names: Myron and Polykleitos are those best known in the art-historical record, though Hageladas, Pythagoras, and Naukydes are among others evidently in demand at Olympia and elsewhere. These sculptors gave added value to the already considerable prestige of having a statue dedicated at Olympia – which as a site became a showcase of skill in epinikian commissions (Pausanias is disdainful of those statues on view at Delphi, as not acknowledged by 'the majority of mankind': 10.9.1).

By the late fourth century BC the Altis contained a dense concentration of commemorated victors. Whether these statues were intended as dedications to Zeus or as honours to mortal success is a topic which briefly concerned Pausanias (5.21.1; 5.25.1), but it is possible that they were both at once. (Exceptionally, the Eleans gave one boy wrestler the permission to put up a statue of his trainer: Pausanias 6.3.6.) Certainly they were serious gifts, with a life-size figure in the fourth century BC costing around 3,000 drachmas – over three times the average annual earnings of an artisan – and a chariot-group a good deal more. Funds might come from the athlete, his relatives, or his city-state. Though statues could be dedicated many years in retrospect, commissions might be undertaken on the spot. The sculptor Pythagoras, though originating from Rhegium in South Italy, must have had some kind of workshop-base at Olympia: his epinikian statues are recorded at almost every Olympiad between 484 and 452 BC (his presence is attested at Delphi, too).

And how much, ultimately, were these statues worth as commemorative objects? We get some idea from a minor epic related by Pausanias with regard to the statue of an early fifth-century BC champion from Thasos called Theagenes (6.11.4). It seems that beyond his victory in the Olympic boxing of 480 BC, and in the *pankration* of the following Olympiad, Theagenes triumphed elsewhere in various athletic disciplines, gaining over a thousand prizes but also making enemies. When Theagenes died, one of these enemies came each night to flog his honorific statue, as if inflicting posthumous revenge. But the statue of Theagenes eventually fell off its pedestal, killing the assailant. The statue was then prosecuted, convicted on a charge of homicide, and 'drowned' in the sea as punishment. But then the island of Thasos suffered a crop failure. Apollo's oracle at Delphi blamed this on the abuse of the image of Theagenes. In the end, fishermen recovered the statue of Theagenes, and the image was re-dedicated – and thereafter venerated respectfully. It was, as Pausanias relates, not only a wondrous piece of art, but also 'wonder-working' or *thaumaturgic* – capable of imparting strength, health, and good fortune to those who came into its presence.

Several other Olympic victors were formally hero-ized in this manner. Philippos of Croton, a victor at the Olympiad of 520 BC, was honoured with a hero-chapel after his death in battle, and venerated for his surpassing beauty (Herodotus 5.47). Kleomedes of Astypalaia, though denied victory in the boxing at the 492 BC Olympiad – because he killed his opponent – and des-pite a subsequent fit of madness that caused the deaths of sixty schoolchildren (Pausanias 6.9.6–7), was likewise paid heroic honours, sanctioned by the Delphic Oracle. The boxer Euthymos of Locri, three times winner in the Olympic boxing, in 484, 476, and 472 BC (and therefore qualifying for an 'iconic' portrait by Pythagoras in 472), was revered as a demigod while he was still alive; as was Polydamas of Skotoussa, the Olympic *pankration*-victor of 408 BC whose prodigious reputation we have already encountered. The statue of Polydamas erected in the Altis was by Lysippos, 'court-sculptor' to Alexander the Great *c*.330 BC, so it must have been a retrospective commission. The very size of Polydamas when alive was enough to make him seem as though he belonged to an earlier breed of hero-types, like Homer's characters; and Lysippos was fond of working on the colossal scale. In any case, the epinikian statue of Polydamas at Olympia had a potency all of its own: touching it was said to cure fevers (Lucian, *Assembly of the Gods* 12).

The Paramountcy of Winning

It is probably redundant now to conclude that winning was of paramount importance at the ancient Olympics. Unlike some other festivals (such as the Panathenaic Games), there were no prizes for runners-up; no silver or bronze positions as today. Still, victory was not to be gained at any cost – at least, not by any *financial* cost. As Pausanias records (5.21.2–18), there was a history of cheating at Olympia from the early fourth century BC, when a Thessalian boxer called Eupolos was caught offering bribes to his several opponents – one of whom was a victor at the previous Olympiad. From the penalty-fines imposed on all guilty parties by the *Hellanodikai*, penitential statues were levied, and set up in a very conspicuous area (between the Metroon and the entrance to the Stadium). According to Pausanias, these statues were called *Zanes*, meaning 'Zeuses' in the Elean dialect; and to judge from some of their bases (excavated and still to be seen *in situ* at Olympia), it seems they were figures of Zeus brandishing his thunderbolt. Pausanias notes a cautionary sentiment inscribed: '*victory is to be achieved by speed of feet and strength of body, not with cash*'. But this warning, and the overt, long-standing disgrace of miscreants, did not deter further incidents of bribery and subterfuge: the *Zanes* multiplied (though admittedly their number in total is not great: just sixteen bases survive).

Resort to cheating might be expected when winning carried such high stakes. But was losing such a disgrace? We do not know whether at Olympia runners who trailed in a race were liable to be abused or even attacked – at the Panathenaic Games, it seems, spectators were licensed to do just that. Pindar alludes to the need for losers to creep home surreptitiously, in order to avoid the gibes and brickbats from their scornful fellow-citizens. But at least the unsuccessful athlete might be good for a few laughs. The *Greek Anthology* contains a number of satiric epigrams aimed at inadequate performers: for example, a boxer called Apis, whose opponents set up a statue to him 'because he never hurt anyone' (11.80); or Marcus the plodding triallist for the race in armour, who by midnight had failed to complete his race, and was locked in the stadium because the groundsmen mistook him for a statue (and by morning poor Marcus had still not reached the finishing-line . . . 11.85).

These celebrities of failure – mostly ascribed to a Greek wit called Lucillus or Lucillius, writing around the time of Nero in the mid-first century AD – do not amount to much indulgence or forgiveness. Throughout antiquity, what mattered in athletic contests was always the winning, not the taking part. The upholding of that ethos is made perfectly clear in one of the most remarkable 'agonistic' inscriptions to have survived from the ancient world, the dedication made at Rome by Marcus Aurelius Asclepiades of Alexandria. It was in the late second century AD when this Marcus put up a statue in honour of his father. The statue has not survived, but its epigraph can still be read: a lengthy and fastidious text that just briefly salutes Asclepiades senior – and goes on to trumpet the importance of Marcus first as an organizer and official of athletic events, then the glories of his preceding career in active competition. Marcus, we learn, was a specialist in the *pankration*, and this is the considerable distinction he claims as a *pankratiastês*:

> I was the invincible, immovable [*asynexôstos*], matchless victor around the athletic circuit [*periodonikês*] – winning every contest that I entered. I never challenged; no one ever dared to challenge me. I never ended a contest with a draw, nor disputed any decision. I never retired from a bout nor failed to turn up; I never gained victory thanks to imperial favour, nor in any newly-concocted [*kainoi*] games, but won my honours in the sandpit of every meeting which I entered, correctly going through all the preliminary procedures [*propeira*]. I competed in three lands – Italy, Greece and Asia – and won the *pankration* events at all the following festivals: the Olympics at Pisa, in the 240th Olympiad, [i.e. AD 181], and the Pythian Games at Delphi; twice at the Isthmian, twice at the Nemean Games (on the second occasion my opponents withdrew), and also at the Shield

Games of Hera at Argos; at the Capitoline Games of
Rome twice – the second time, with opponents pull-
ing out after the first drawing of lots [*kleros*]; the
Eusebia Games of Puteoli, twice (second time,
opponents withdrew after first drawing of lots), the
Sebasta Games at Naples, twice (second time,
opponents withdrew after second drawing of lots) . . .

(*IG* XIV.1102)

And so it goes on. For a span of six years, it seems
there was hardly any athletic meeting around the
Mediterranean at which Marcus did not carry off honours. At the age of 25, he says, he retired; and he specifies
that one reason for his retirement was the incidence of
jealousy generated by his victories. Marcus may have
been aware of an eccentric dictum issued by the sixth-
century BC sage Pythagoras, to the effect that it was
preferable *not* to win in athletic contests, if envy should
be forestalled (Porphyry, *Life of Pythagoras* 15). But this
was as Pindar and all the epinikian poets and artists had
emphasized: the winner's glorious life was a truly envi-
able state of existence. It was an irresistible pull. As
Marcus concludes: 'Years later, I gave in to the urge –
and won the *pankration* at the sixth Olympiad of the
Olympics at my home-town, Alexandria.'

5

THE POLITICS OF CONTEST

Perusing the victory-lists of the ancient Olympics can be a poignant experience. So many names once tagged to the splendid status of 'deathless renown' – now nothing more than names. But to study the entries with a Mediterranean gazetteer at one's elbow is instructive. The victor's name is always linked to the *polis* which claimed him as its own. Trace those proprietorial city-states on the map, and a demographic pattern of Olympic success soon becomes apparent.

So, from 776 to 732 BC, winners are drawn just from the immediate region of Olympia itself – the western Peloponnese. From 732 to 696 BC, this area widens to include the rest of the Peloponnese. Then, throughout the seventh century BC, victors are mostly supplied by Athens and Sparta. A harbinger of glory for the Greek colonies in the western Mediterranean is also signalled in the seventh century, with Daippos of Croton crowned for the Olympic boxing in 672 BC; and at one archaic Olympiad, we are told, no fewer than seven sprinters from the same colony outstripped everyone else in the *stade*-race (Strabo, *Geography* 6.1.12). But it is the sixth century which really belongs to the Greek settlers in South Italy and Sicily, with Syracuse, Himera, Locri, and others joining Croton in the archive of illustrious athletic provenance.

Parts of central and northern Greece, such as Thessaly, also make their mark at Olympia during the sixth century. Subsequently we enter the 'Classic' period of Olympic victory-commemoration in poetry and sculpture. From *c*.500 until the subjection of Greece to Philip II of Macedon (after the battle of Chaeronea in 338 BC), the picture is one of a truly 'Panhellenic' sharing of honours at Olympia, with city-states from virtually all the dispersed Greek territories, even tiny islands such as Astypalaia, gaining some victory or other. Thereafter begins the eastward shift in athletic ascendancy, accelerating after the death (in 323 BC) of Philip II's son and successor, Alexander the Great. As the momentum of Alexander's conquests had carried Greek values deep into the heartlands of Asia, so we find the Olympia victory-record increasingly dominated by athletes from Greek-speaking communities in coastal Anatolia, Phoenicia, Syria, and Egypt – above all, from Alexander's eponymous foundation in the Nile Delta, Alexandria.

The Roman takeover of Greece in the second century BC, and the consolidation of Roman power in Asia Minor and the Middle East by the first century AD, did little to affect this oriental bias of Olympic victory; if anything, it became stronger. Scholars like to speak of a 'Second Sophistic' occurring in the Roman Empire, around the time of Hadrian's rule (AD 117–138), meaning a revival of Greek intellectual traditions. It would be equally apt to invoke a 'Second Agonistic' for this period too, with local athletic festivals proliferating especially in the cities of the Eastern Mediterranean seaboard – and those same cities handsomely proud of accomplishment at Olympia, to judge from the epigraphic trail.

What are we to make of this pattern? It attests, certainly, to the remarkable resilience and magnetism of the ancient Olympics as a festival occasion – one that survived at least two major 'regime changes', without radically compromising its traditional format or religious *raison d'être*. It says a good deal, too, about the essential coherence of 'Greekness', or Hellenicity, as a concept, if not a reality. The Altis at Olympia was a communal sanctuary maintained for sacred use by all Greeks, wherever they belonged in the Greek-inhabited world, or *oikoumenê*. Olympia was, in Pindar's view, a God-given enclave of ultimate trust and accessibility: 'a place open to all' (*Olympian* 6.63).

Or was it? We know well enough from modern Olympic history that faith in lofty ideals is not enough to guarantee the inoculation of sport against political disputes. Our task in this chapter is to construct a political history of the ancient Olympics, from their supposed beginning in 776 BC to their supposed closure in AD 393. What happened before 776 BC must wait for the following chapter; here, for the sake of order, over a thousand years of history are divided into three broad phases. We shall end, however, by considering a question of social rather than political significance. When Pindar says 'open to all', does he really mean that *anyone* – from tyrant to donkey-driver – could compete at the Games?

Phase I: Fighting for Control of the Sanctuary

As Chapter 6 will explain, Olympia was not founded as a Panhellenic centre, rather reinvented as such in the fifth century BC. On the evidence of votive offerings, the sanctuary was not much frequented by Greeks beyond the immediate locality during the previous ninth to seventh centuries; and the domination of the victory-list by Peloponnesian athletes from 776 to 696 BC is probably due to the fact that only Peloponnesian athletes competed. Nevertheless, struggles to control the site, and efforts to extend its religious 'reach' abroad, can both be traced in the obscure protohistory of Olympia.

When Strabo identifies the location of Olympia as part of his *Geography*, composed in the early first century AD, he says simply that the sanctuary lies in the valley of the Alpheios, 'where the river flows through the lands of Pisatis and Triphylia' (8.3.12). Neither of these place-names can be said to have great resonance in the pages of Greek history. 'Pisatis' means the territory of a habitation called Pisa, which once stood very close to the sanctuary. Taking the road that runs northwards today, visitors will find signs to 'Ancient Pisa' – though very little to see of it, for reasons which will soon become clear. What of Triphylia? The name translates as 'the territory of three tribes', and its area appears to have extended down to Pylos – though since there are several places in the western Peloponnese called Pylos, this may not be helpful information. One of these, a Mycenaean site of c.1600–1200 BC near Chora in Messenia, was optimistically titled 'the Palace of Nestor' by its excavator, Carl Blegen. But when Homer's Nestor delves into his long memory for stories of youthful valour in these parts (*Iliad* 11. 671–761), it seems as though the old warrior has in mind a 'Triphylian Pylos' to be located somewhere along the coast between the rivers Alpheios and Neda, perhaps at modern Kakovatos.

Nestor tells of an incident of tit-for-tat cattle-raiding with people who dwelt north of the Alpheios. He specifies who they were: Eleans, from the fertile area whose capital was Elis, up by the River Peneios. 'Elis' can also refer to the wider area: it was one of those parts of the Peloponnese occupied in the late second millennium BC by incomers from the north whom we traditionally classify as the Dorians, though Homer prefers to speak of 'Achaeans'. Nestor shows no awareness of any special athletic festival at Olympia, though he does mention holding a highly carnivorous pre-battle feast and sacrifice in honour of Zeus and other Olympian deities, right by the banks of the Alpheios. His allusion to the Eleans, however, is significant. The three tribes that once inhabited Triphylia are named by Strabo as the Eleans, the Minyans, and the Epeians (Nestor's dispute, it turns out, is chiefly with the latter). Historically there is no doubt that the Eleans eventually prevailed as political overlords of the area.

How they did so is not well documented; or rather, since history tends to be written by the victorious, we rely upon a version of events presented by the Eleans – a heavily mythologized version at that. Nestor's tale suggests how precious were the meadowlands of the Alpheios for pasture and stock-breeding. Triphylia was also proverbial for its fertile land. Was Olympia, then, a politically coveted place because it happened to be the shrine where tithes and thanksgivings were offered by the region's farmers? Or was it rather, as Strabo believed (8.3.30), on account of a more particular religious significance of the site – the reputation of Olympia as not only an altar *to* Zeus, but an altar used *by* the god for divulging to mortals his divine purpose, an oracle.

Since it was in the nature of ancient oracles to surpass mortal understanding, we can expect not to comprehend very much about how this oracle at Olympia functioned. Unlike that of Apollo at Delphi, very few literary citations of messages received from the Olympic oracle are known. It is only thanks to Pindar that we learn of a mythical origin for Olympia's privileged access to the will of Zeus: and as recounted in his *Olympian Ode* 6, this is simply a charming fable of somewhat predictable structure. A god (Apollo) impregnates an Arcadian nymph (Evadne), who abandons the resultant offspring in a bed of purple pansies at the foot of the Hill of Kronos. The infant, called Iamos, is fed on honey by snakes; flourishes to manhood, learns the art of prophecy from his erstwhile father, and is eventually appointed by Apollo as a seer at Olympia. When Herakles establishes a programme of athletics at the site, this oracle is already in operation at the altar of Zeus.

Centuries after Pindar, inscriptions concerning the sanctuary staff at Olympia mention 'descendants of Iamos', *Iamidai*, functioning as 'prophets' (*manteis*) at the site. Evidently these were life-long and hereditary posts. But inscriptions also tell of another family of Elean soothsayers, the *Klytiadai*, or 'descendants of Klytios', sharing the oracular duties. The Roman writer Cicero understood that both *Iamidai* and *Klytiadai* held office at Olympia (*On Divination* 1.41); confusingly, however, Herodotus talks of *Iamidai* and *Telliadai*, while yet another source (Philostratos, *Life of Apollonius* 5.25) thinks there to be three prophetic families involved. Whoever and how many they were, evidently a separate guide or 'interpreter' (*exêgêtês*) was required to make plain the divine information collected by these seers. Just such a 'local expert' was probably the source of the

Olympic lore related by Pausanias; and it is Pausanias who mentions that one of the *Iamidai* extended the art of divination by inspecting the entrails of sacrificial dogs (6.2.4).

This oracle, as anticipated, remains the most mysterious aspect of ancient Olympia, and one which archaeology is unlikely ever to illuminate. But some inkling of its significance is necessary if we are to comprehend how Olympia eventually claimed Panhellenic status – and, in particular, a reputation for monitoring the military affairs of the Greek city-states. Just what sort of messages came through from Zeus via the *Iamidai* and their kind?

Herodotus leaves an important clue. We gather from his narratives of archaic Greek history that the Olympic seers could travel with their foreknowledge, as part of an army's *équipe* (see Herodotus 5.44; 9.33; 9.37). 'Chaplains' does not really describe this itinerant role: they were prophets empowered to forecast nothing less than victory or defeat. If that was indeed the power they wielded, then we are already some way to understanding why trophies of arms and armour constitute such a large proportion of votive dedications made at Olympia from *c.*800–400 BC. In this period of hoplite and naval warfare among the Greeks, or between Greeks and non-Greeks, victory was customarily regarded as god-given, and brought with it the obligation of devoting one-tenth of the spoils as thanksgiving to the god. So long as the inspired vicars of Zeus at Olympia were 'getting it right' in their strategic predictions, then the sanctuary would burgeon with votive rewards.

How or whether the oracle at Olympia was related to the other oracle of Zeus at Dodona, up in Epirus, is not clear. But an intriguing liaison with Apollo's oracle at Delphi is implicit in the story told by Herodotus about Teisamenos, one of the *Iamidai* family, who asks Apollo about his chances of having children. On being told that he is destined to win 'five of the greatest contests', Teisamenos sets about training for the pentathlon – and very nearly wins it at the next Olympiad. But since he does not actually win, there is a re-interpretation of the oracular message, with the Spartans proposing that the *agônes* referred to at Delphi must be those of war, not athletics. They accordingly bid for the services of Teisamenos, whose price is that both he and his brother must be made Spartan citizens. It is an unprecedented demand, but the Spartans concede. And it turns out to be a concession well worth making. Teisamenos accompanies the Spartan army first to the battle of Plataea against the Persians, and then to four further engagements. In all five 'contests' he is on the victorious side (Herodotus 9. 33–5).

This may be as much as we can say about the Olympic seers: that they took an active, pragmatic interest in military affairs. The potential political importance of such intervention would have been sufficient by itself. But there was also, of course, the tendency to view athletic success as symbolic of success in other endeavours, including public life: so Olympia became invested with yet further political value. Herodotus tells how, for instance, an Athenian aristocrat called Kylon was so emboldened by his victory in the *diaulos* foot-race at the 35th Olympiad (in 640 BC) that he attempted a *coup d'état* at Athens (5.71). A century or so later, another Athenian aristocrat, Kimon, gained the remarkable distinction of not only winning the Olympic four-horse chariot-race three times, but doing so with the same team of mares on each occasion. As Herodotus records (6.35–6), this Kimon discovered exactly what an Olympic victory could be worth in terms of a political trade-off. Consigned into exile by the ruling tyrant of Athens, Kimon negotiated his return by agreeing to 'transfer' his second Olympic *tethrippon* title to that tyrant, Peisistratos. Thus Peisistratos shrewdly joined the roll-call of archaic Greek tyrants victorious at Olympia: the Orthagorids of Sikyon, the Kypselids of Corinth, and others.

As we have seen chariot-racing was always the event associated with the autocratic or politically ambitious, though the history of the Diagorid dynasty of Rhodes (see p. 153) and certain other Olympic champions proves that athletes of various disciplines could pursue political careers in their home towns. What concerns us here, though, is how Olympia itself survived a series of disputes over its possession and administration.

The local wrangle between Elis and Pisa flared up intermittently after the Olympic foundation date of 776 BC. At one point in the eighth or seventh century, it seems, the Pisatans invited an Argive monarch, Pheidon, to assist them in ousting the Eleans, and asserted control over a series of Olympiads – which the Eleans later annulled. (Though it has been speculated that Pheidon left his mark by bringing to Olympia the cult of Hera, the principal deity of Argos.) With Spartan support, the Eleans recovered control of Olympia, or their share in it, and appear to have prevailed conclusively over Pisa *c.*470 BC, when the Temple of Zeus was funded, according to Pausanias (5.10.2), from booty seized by the Eleans in their outright destruction of Pisa. 'Pisa' would continue to be used as a poetic toponym for the Olympia site, but no longer existed as a settlement.

From the late sixth century BC onwards the political possessiveness of Elis towards Olympia is manifest in the devices and designs of Elean coin issues. The eagle of Zeus, the thunderbolt of Zeus, the figure of Winged Victory with an olive wreath – these symbolic elements linked Elis firmly to Olympia's cult and the Olympic Games. (A motif based on the colossal cult image of Zeus by Pheidias would later join the numismatic repertoire.) Yet the Eleans were sensitive to the issue of their impartial management of the Olympic Games. We can presume as much from the story in Herodotus (2.160; see also Diodorus Siculus 1.95) about a delegation sent from Elis to the Egyptian pharaoh Psammis (Psammetichus II) early in the sixth century BC. The Eleans were confident that they were overseeing a competitive programme that was as well regulated as they could imagine: was there any scope, they wondered, for improvement? The Egyptians enquired whether the Eleans allowed their own people to compete; and, on learning this to be the case, recommended that the Eleans should stay out of the contests.

The Eleans did not heed that wise advice. All the same, they presided over a meeting-place that was ever more conspicuously open to 'statements' by the many independent Greek cities frequenting Olympia for its oracle, rites, or athletic trials. The monumental impact of this political self-expression is difficult to gauge at the site today: we have to imagine the glittering stacks of captured arms and armour that once festooned the area as war-trophies, even in the Stadium. But certain excavated features assist the imagining. One such feature is the 'Terrace of the Treasuries', laid out on a cutting in the Hill of Kronos, with an eminent view over the Altis (and the Stadium too, in its earlier alignments). 'Little temples' (*naiskoi*), 'houses' (*oikoi*), or in one case perhaps just an altar – the dozen structures occupying this ridge have not all been definitively identified either by type or sponsoring city. Archaeologists agree that the west and east ends of the terrace are occupied by buildings erected by Sikyon and Gela respectively, with Sikyon setting the precedent according to Pausanias (6.19.1), but Gela offering the oldest surviving foundations (*c.*570 BC).

For Pausanias it was Myron, the tyrant of Sikyon, who initiated the raising of a double-chambered 'treasury', or *thesauros*, after his victory in the chariot-race at the 33rd Olympiad of 648 BC. Pausanias goes on to describe the assortment of 'treasures' on display here. There were the chamber walls themselves, fashioned out of bronze – an imposing bequest of metal from Myron and the Sikyonians. Within, there were three *diskoi*, usable in pentathlon contests; a shield and pieces of armour, dedicated as a victory-tithe from battle with another Greek community; and, among other curiosities, a statue of Apollo, and a gold-handled dagger said to have belonged to Olympia's mythical founding-figure, Pelops.

From this selective inventory by Pausanias we understand why these dainty buildings were called 'treasuries': they were storerooms of booty, votive gifts, and *objets d'art*. Other Panhellenic sanctuaries, notably Delphi, also made space for such storerooms. But of course very many Greek cities go unrepresented here. The *polis*-names associated with the Terrace of Treasuries at Olympia are usually reckoned as Sikyon, Syracuse, Epidamnos, Byzantium, Sybaris, Cyrene, Selinus, Metapontion, Megara, and Gela. Of these, only Sikyon and Megara belong to the Greek mainland. Epidamnos was a colony on the Adriatic coast (now Durres in Albania); Byzantium a colony on the Bosphorus (later Constantinople, now Turkish Istanbul); Cyrene a colony in North Africa (now the east coast of Libya); the rest, settlements planted in South Italy and Sicily.

The far-off location of these colonial outposts adds credibility to the suggestion (implicit from some ancient sources) that the Treasuries served as 'club houses' or meeting points for visitors from abroad, especially the envoys (*theôroi*, 'onlookers') sent as official representatives to the sanctuary (for example, to consult the oracle). Moreover, the geographical spread of these colonies – to the north, south, west, and east of the Peloponnese – is often invoked as a sign of Olympia's Panhellenic aspirations. But the erection of the Treasuries, largely a sixth-century BC development, predates the ideology of Panhellenism at Olympia. And if we care to refine the ethnic identity of the Treasuries' founding cities, it becomes apparent that they are all more or less connected by the factor of Dorian or Achaean descent. The other ethnic sub-groups of the Greeks – Aeolians, Ionians, and the 'Pelasgian' inhabitants of Arcadia – are absent.

Stories about how Greek colonies were founded are notoriously romantic, but it is worth noting at this point one recurring element – the part played by successful athletes. Cyrene, for instance, was founded *c.*630 BC by (Dorian) people from Thera, with Spartan support: 'Spartan support' for the expedition chiefly consisting, it seems, in the loan of a three-times Olympic victor called Chionis (Pausanias 3.14.3). If Olympia's heroes were involved in colonial initiatives, all the more reason for the eventual colonies to keep up links with the sanctuary (in the Sikyonian Treasury Pausanias also glimpsed a votive dedication by one such athlete-pioneer, the elder Miltiades (son of Kypselos), whose victory in the

Olympic chariot-race *c.*560 BC had 'qualified' him to annexe the Thracian Chersonese – territory we know as the Gallipoli peninsula: see Herodotus 6.36). And Pindar adds a further slant on this process when he hints (*Olympian* 6.6) that Iamid seers from Olympia accompanied the colonists from Corinth who in the late eighth century BC set out to establish themselves at Syracuse on the coast of Sicily. Olympia, then, was not simply an arena to which Greek colonies dispatched formidable athletes as signs of their material prosperity. The Olympic oracle, like that of Delphi, was itself a seminal part of the colonizing process.

Naturally the process was mythologized. So we find the story of how Alpheios was once an Arcadian hunter, who fell for a nymph called Arethusa. Arethusa fled to Syracuse, where she transformed into a fountain; hence Alpheios became a river, flowing into and over the 'Sicilian Sea' to find his beloved (Pausanias 5.7.2). Beyond such tales, the prosaic factors of Mediterranean topography may be invoked. To this day, the easiest way of reaching Olympia is from the west, by sea. The route over land from Athens may be picturesque to modern travellers, but is an undeniably tough journey on foot and was considered so in antiquity (see Xenophon, *Memorabilia* 3.15.5). In terms of access, then, Olympia was really not very remote from places such as Syracuse and Metapontion. And sentimentally, for certain colonial foundations, going to Olympia must have been like a sort of homecoming.

Phase II: The Rhetoric of *Homonoia*

Bickering between themselves could almost be described as a full-time activity of the Greek city-states. For as often as Greek history chronicles the formation of leagues among various cities, it also documents the dissolution of those alliances, or the outbreak of fresh rivalries. Hoplite warfare may be seen as the brusque mechanism by which such inter-Greek hostilities were settled. In this ambience of endemic mutual suspicion, it is perhaps predictable that only the pressure of a great threat from outside the Greek world could compel the Greeks into a policy of united action.

That threat came from the Asian empire of the Medes and Persians, which in the mid-sixth century BC had begun to expand towards the Mediterranean. Under Cyrus II and Darius, Greek settlements along the Ionian coast were absorbed into the Persian sphere during the sixth century. Then Darius ordered an invasion of the Greek mainland. Guided by a renegade displaced after the end of tyranny at Athens, Persian forces made a huge amphibious landing at Marathon, on the east coast of Attica, in 490 BC. The tale of how Athens met this challenge to its newly fledged democracy was stirringly scripted by Herodotus (6.94–120), emphasizing what a close-run encounter it was, and how only one other Greek *polis*, Boeotian Plataea, had come to the support of Athens at Marathon. Within a decade, however, the Persians – now commanded in person by Xerxes – were back. This time they descended upon Attica via Macedon, and succeeded in occupying the very Akropolis of Athens. At last – not so much to save Athens, but because the next Persian objective was to conquer the Peloponnese – a coalition of Greek forces was assembled: a *symmachia*, or 'fellowship in fighting'. The decisive battles were fought at sea off the island of Salamis in 480 BC, and on land at Plataea and Mykale in 479. Chief-in-command at Plataea was a Spartan; and a monument later set up at Delphi listed 31 Greek city-states as contributing to the victory.

When one of the coalition generals, the Athenian Themistokles, came to Olympia for the post-war Games of 476 BC, he was given a tumultous ovation (Plutarch, *Themistokles* 17) – eclipsing the athletics, and probably also causing some embarrassment to the Eleans, whose own mustering against the Persians had been rather feeble. For a time, it seemed as though the Greeks collectively had learned the lesson of co-operating. One inscription from Olympia implies the creation, in 476 or shortly thereafter, of an arbitration tribunal convened at the sanctuary to settle disputes between Greek states: Boeotians, Athenians, and Thessalians were involved in two early decisions of this court.

But Olympia and the *periodos* of 'Panhellenic' festivals did not avert the most grievous episode of discord between the Greeks – the cumulative turmoil known as the Peloponnesian War. Lasting from 431 to 404 BC, this conflict was presented by its prime historian,

Thucydides, as essentially the collision between Athens and Sparta. But few Greek cities were unaffected, not even the colonies (one notorious turn of events was the Athenian attempt upon Syracuse in 415–413 BC – a venture headed by Alcibiades, riding on his recent Olympic success).

The Olympic Games were celebrated all the same; or even more keenly, perhaps, since the practice of offering monumental thanks for victory at Olympia stayed intact. The possibilities of using such monuments vindictively are well illustrated by a work of art from Olympia which, out of context, seems like the very image of sweetness and light – the 'Nike of Paionios' (**Fig. 35**). Excavated in 1875, this statue is usually appreciated for its sculptor's ability to give solid marble a pneumatic, gravity-resistant grace; intuitively we can see why the man who made it, Paionios of Mende, made sure he was mentioned in the accompanying inscription. But the piece has political piquancy too. Pausanias informs us (5.24.3) that in the Altis of the Temple of Zeus at Olympia, the Spartans had erected a statue of Zeus in gratitude for their success

35. The 'Winged Victory' (*Nike*) of Paionios, marble figure. Height 2.11 m, originally placed on a triangular base, height 8.81 m by the southeast corner of the Temple of Zeus. A double inscription on the base says that the Messenians and Naupaktians dedicated the statue with 'a tithe arising from battle' (the enemy is not specified); and that Paionios of Mende (in Chalkidike) 'was victorious' in gaining the commission for this and some of the other temple sculptures.

in quelling a rebellion by the Messenians – whom the Spartans had made their subjects – at a date probably in the first half of the fifth century BC. Some decades later, in 425–424, there was revenge for the Messenians. With Athenian assistance, and in league with exiled kinsfolk at Naupaktos, they captured an entire Spartan garrison on the island of Sphakteria, just off the coast by modern Pylos (see Thucydides 4.2–41). The success of the raid was duly signalled in the Altis of Olympia. Spectacularly so, with an eye-catchingly airborne personification of Victory not only designed to show how much the 'one-tenth' (*dekate*) of captured spoils was worth, but surely also raised so high in order to demean the nearby Spartan statue – and possibly also to obscure the sight of other Spartan trophies affixed to the temple skyline.

The appearance of the Nike of Paionios cannot have done much to improve the deteriorating relations between Sparta and Elis. To recount in detail the various twists of this political falling-out would be tedious: it may be enough to mention that the Eleans tried to ban Spartan athletes from competing at Olympia in 420 BC, after an altercation over territorial influence (Thucydides 5.31, 49), and that Elis and Sparta were at war in 402–401 (Xenophon, *Hellenica* 3.2.23). The durability of local identities in this region was demonstrated when in 371 BC, led by the gifted Boeotian strategist and diplomat Epaminondas, the Arcadian city-states came together, and Spartan power across the Peloponnese weakened (Messenia regaining independence in 369).

The inhabitants of Triphylia and Pisatis were still aware of being Triphylians and Pisatans. Seeing that Elis had no hope of Spartan assistance, they invited the Arcadian League to intervene on their behalf at Olympia. So it happened that Arcadian troops were occupying the site when the 104th Olympiad took place in 364 BC. As Xenophon vividly describes it (*Hellenica* 7.4.28–33), the equestrian events were over, and the pentathlon was under way, when a detachment of Eleans appeared. The Arcadians were lined up along the Kladeos River, with support from 2,000 Argive hoplites and 400 Athenian cavalry. The Eleans surprised them, however, with a determined assault. There was pitched battle actually in the Altis: some soldiers climbed onto the top of the Temple of Zeus and the Council House, and hurled missiles down below. At nightfall, the Arcadians built a stockade from the huts and stalls of the Olympic 'village' by the Alpheios. The Eleans withdrew, having made their point (Olympia belonged to *them*); and, partly because some mercenaries of the Arcadians disgraced themselves by looting the Treasuries, control of Olympia was subsequently restored to Elis by 362.

The Eleans acknowledged the victors of the 364 Games, but labelled it a 'Non-Olympiad' (*Anolympias*), as they had done for the Games held while Olympia was under the sway of Pheidon (Pausanias 6.22.3). Certainly the events of 364 made an absolute mockery of the tradition of the supposedly inviolate Olympic armistice or 'Sacred Truce' – the *ekecheiria*, or 'staying of hands', required to ensure a sixteen-day cessation of hostilities all around Greece while the festival was convened. This was, literally, a much-heralded feature of the Games, with the Eleans dispatching proclaimers around the Greek-speaking world to call for peace during the Olympic 'national assembly', or *panêgyris*. In fact a certain tone of shame is palpable in Greek sources even before the occurrence of the 'battle in the Altis'. While the Peloponnesian War was at its height, *c.*411 BC, the Athenian comic playwright Aristophanes presented his 'anti-war' drama, the *Lysistrata* – whose heroine Lysistrata ('Disbander of Armies') orchestrates a 'sex-strike' at Athens, Sparta, and elsewhere whereby wives withdraw marital favours until their husbands see sense and stop fighting. In one speech, Lysistrata asks male representatives of Athens and Sparta, 'where's Reconciliation [*Diallagê*]? . . . don't you all pour libations at communal altars, for communal deities, like kinsmen [*syngeneis*] at the Olympic Games . . .?'

Herodotus – who expressly chose the gathering at Olympia as the most effective way of making his historical 'Inquiries' known to a Panhellenic audience (Lucian, *Herodotus and Aëtion* 1–4) – had given a definition of 'Hellenicity' that emphasized the sharing of sacred sites and customs (*Histories* 8.144); Plato, too, would stress the role of panegyrical festivals in bringing Greeks together and fostering a sense of ethnic identity (*Republic* 470e). The most passionate pleading for the cause of Panhellenic concord, or *homonoia* ('same-mindedness'), came, however, from a succession of notable Greek orators who used the occasion of the Olympic Games as their rostrum. First of these was the long-lived Sophist Gorgias from Sicily, who came to Olympia in 408 BC. The full text of his Olympic discourse (*Olympikos logos*) has not survived, but in epitome it transpires that Gorgias tried to persuade the Greeks gathered at Olympia not to consider their respective city-states as prizes to be seized by force of arms, and instead to direct their aggressive inclinations towards the territory of the barbarians (Philostratos, *Lives of the Sophists* 493). Notwithstanding the gossip that Gorgias could not even achieve harmony in his own household, let alone the world at large (Plutarch, *Moralia* 144c), this set an influential precedent.

In 388 or 384 BC the Athenian democrat Lysias began his celebrated *Olympiakos* speech with the proposition that Herakles had founded the Olympic Games precisely to promote *homonoia* and curtail factionalism among the Greeks. The rest of the speech can only be described as downright inflammatory, with Lysias virtually urging his listeners to sack the ostentatious pavilions erected in the Olympic village by delegates of Dionysius, the tyrant of Syracuse – which happened to be the home town of Lysias (see also Diodorus Siculus 14.109). Not long after Lysias, another Athenian speechmaker, Isocrates, came to Olympia (*c.*380 BC) to deliver his *Panêgyrikos*, smoothly glorifying the value of the Panhellenic festivals as opportunities to cement friendships and affirm the cultural communion that made Hellas, 'Greece', a precious entity.

Gorgias, Lysias, and Isocrates were stellar performers in the art of rhetoric: their efforts at Olympia may be regarded as so many displays or set-pieces designed to impress. It was no coincidence that the Sophists had already borrowed the athletic jargon of 'entering the lists' (*agônizesthai*: see Plato, *Hippias Minor* 364a); it was natural enough that Gorgias should be honoured at Olympia with a statue – like any victorious athlete, though probably fully robed – complete with inscription attesting excellence (the base has been found: *IvO* 293). 'Intellectual struggle', *agôn peri tês psychês*, claimed its own worth: Isocrates, in particular, liked to think of himself as performing 'mental gymnastics' (*gymnasia tês psychês*). But so long as these distinguished speechmakers came to Olympia, as it were, to distinguish themselves further, we may wonder whether their message of *homonoia* across Hellas was not simply a set 'trope' – a suitable theme of discourse, which once addressed by one great orator at Olympia had to be followed by others for them to prove themselves better.

In this sense it is better to speak of a *rhetoric* of Panhellenic unity at Olympia in the fifth and early fourth centuries BC. The concept of pooling mutual interests was fully aired; there was an altar to 'Unanimity'; and, after the events of 364, a statue of Zeus inscribed 'From the Eleans, for Concord' (*IvO* 260). But the *reality* of inter-Greek co-operation came about only by *force majeure* – that is, the domination of Greece first by Macedon, then Rome.

Phase III: Macedonian Olympia; Roman Olympia

Is Macedonia Greek? The question can be a very sensitive issue of ethnic identity and nomenclature today; in antiquity, too, it was debatable. Geographically the ancient kingdom of Macedon lay between Greece and the Balkans, encompassing mountains and plains above the Gulf of Thermai; ethnically its population had some Dorian affiliations, mixed with Thracians and Illyrians; culturally, too, its status (in Greek eyes) was uncertain. When one Macedonian monarch, Alexander I, arrived at Olympia in the early fifth century BC to compete in the *stade*-race, other competitors protested that, as a 'barbarian', he was not allowed to compete. The *Hellanodikai* had to interpret their role as 'Greek judges' quite literally, and judge whether Alexander qualified for Greekness (Herodotus 5.22). The king alleged his descent from a family of Argos, and was permitted to run – but although he finished in equal first place, and invited Pindar to his court, his name does not appear in the victory-lists.

Alexander belonged to a dynasty which claimed descent from Herakles. After his death in *c.*450 BC, successive rulers from this dynasty consolidated Macedon as a powerful autocracy while the Greek city-states were locked in conflict either with the Persians or with each other. By the mid-fourth century, Philip II of Macedon was ready to assert a Macedonian claim to safeguard 'Greece' against 'barbarians'. This claim was primarily backed by a large, innovative, and professional army, which the citizen-hoplites of the independent Greek city-states stood little chance of resisting. But Philip also aimed to impress upon the Greeks his own impeccable Hellenic credentials. He was represented at Olympia in 356 BC, duly winning the horse-race; later he added two victories in chariot-racing, which he commemorated on some of his coin-issues.

Philip's decisive victory over Greek forces at Chaeronea in 338 BC was followed two years later by his assassination. It was probably his successor, young Alexander 'the Great', who saw through the completion of a conspicuous monument to Philip at Olympia – the circular *tholos* building whose base can still be seen in the Altis precincts, close to the Temple of Hera. Marble Ionic columns ringed a shrine that contained a set of gold-and-ivory statues of Philip, Alexander, Philip's father Amyntas and mother Eurydice, and Philip's Greek wife Olympias – all executed by Leochares, the most sought-after Greek sculptor of the time. A sort of apotheosis was clearly intended.

So far as we know, Alexander himself never visited Olympia. Olympia had to content itself with delegated imagery of the dashing commander, busy leading Macedonian conquests across Asia. A painter called Aëtion exhibited his picture of the wedding of Alexander to the Bactrian princess Roxane at Olympia; one of the *Hellanodikai*, apparently, was so taken by this scene that he offered its artist the hand of *his* daughter in marriage

(Lucian, *Herodotus and Aëtion* 4). Despite Alexander's absence, however, the sanctuary appears to have benefited from Macedonian investment. The Altis was handsomely enclosed by walls in this period, and the 'Echo Colonnade' added along the east side provided elegant shelter for spectators of events held within the Altis.

Alexander's death in 323 BC left a number of his chiefs-of-staff in position to create their own dynasties in Asia and around the eastern Mediterranean. The establishment of these kingdoms – the Antigonids in Macedon and Greece, the Ptolemies in Egypt, the Seleucids in Syria, later the Attalids at Pergamum, and so on – basically explains why the Olympic victory-lists become more cosmopolitan from *c.*300 BC onwards; though it is interesting to note that cities in the west-central Peloponnese enjoy a new run of success at this time, too.

The period of 323–31 BC is customarily termed 'the Hellenistic Age'. It is worth remembering that 'Hellenistic' strictly implies only that Greek was used as a language of convenience by non-Greek peoples. An understanding of Greek was probably all that became required of competitors coming to Olympia from Asia, Egypt, or the Middle East. If the sanctuary was to flourish, it could not afford to impose a *cordon sanitaire* of ethnic purity.

Ptolemy II Philadelphos was honoured together with his wife (and sister) Arsinoe by vertiginous statues at Olympia *c.*270 BC; the king's mistress, Belistiche, won a chariot victory in 264. The Olympic *palaistra* constructed around this time may have been made possible by Ptolemaic munificence; in any case, the athletic facilities back in the Ptolemies' capital at Alexandria were beginning to produce a steady supply of successful Olympic contenders.

In short, Olympia and the Olympics were in good shape when Roman armies descended upon Greece in the second century BC.

One of the Roman generals who inflicted great damage upon the Macedonians was L. Aemilius Paullus. Significantly, Paullus chose to mark his victory at the battle of Pydna in 167 BC with a dedicatory monument at Delphi – and also made a pilgrimage to Olympia, where he gave sacrificial thanksgiving at the Temple of Zeus. The Roman historian Livy, not generally inclined to applaud undue reverence for Greek works of art, relates how impressed Paullus was by the sight of the colossal Zeus *Nikephoros* within the temple (*Ab urbe condita* 45.28). Both the monument at Delphi and the sacrifice at Olympia augured well for the Panhellenic sanctuaries under Roman control.

Did the Romans preside over decay at Olympia? Historians have tended to view it that way, lamenting the absence of stories, poems, or statues to do with extraordinary Olympic performers, and dwelling gleefully on the accounts of Nero at Olympia – extraordinary for the wrong reasons (Nero apparently won some six or seven events). But an impartial assessment of what the Romans did for Olympia would have to pronounce in their favour. Not only were the facilities for athletes and spectators substantially improved. The *ethos* of the Games was both retained and extended. As Pausanias proves, the studiously 'Hellenic' basis of Olympia's traditions was, if anything, stronger in the second century AD than it had been before. At the same time, participation at Olympia was also more cosmopolitan than ever. 'Asterix at the Olympic Games' is a comic-strip fantasy – but it is not entirely fantastic to imagine an athlete arriving at Olympia from Romanized Gaul. One of the last recorded names of victors at Olympia is that of Varazdates, a Persian from Armenia who won the boxing title in 385 AD.

Even Nero's laughable Olympic reputation is now subject to revision. Nero was loathed by his opponents at Rome for promoting athletics and gymnasia in Italy, and suspected also of pilfering statues from Olympia (Pausanias 5.26.3). But archaeologically it has become clear that Nero was a munificent benefactor to the cause of athletics in Greece, and funded an athletes' club house at Olympia (beyond the southwest corner of the Altis: it was completed under Domitian in AD 84). Another 'villain' of history, King Herod of Judaea, was also generous: in 12 BC, he rescued the sanctuary from financial straits by personally subsidizing the festival (Josephus, *The Jewish War* 1.426–7). The Eleans titled him *agônothetês* in gratitude, and made a practice of honouring potential or actual Roman patrons with statues at Olympia, including the emperor Tiberius (*IvO* 220) and his adopted son Germanicus (*IvO* 221) – both of whom, following centuries'-old tradition, gained victory in chariot-racing.

Evidence that the Romans actually removed statues from Olympia is thin. Very few original bronzes of illustrious athletes are known to have been hoisted from their Greek settings. There is some literary evidence: for instance, the statue of a wrestler called Cheimon, done by Naukydes, was allegedly taken from Argos by Nero to decorate his 'Golden House' in Rome (Pliny, *Natural History* 34.84). Otherwise, some sort of legalized trade in athletic masterpieces may be implied by several bronzes recovered from the Mediterranean sea-bed (see Figs. 6 and 14). But the Romans mostly settled for marble copies. Near the Baths of Trajan at Rome we learn of a guildhall of athletes that commissioned copies of Greek athletic statues (*IG* XIV.1109). Providing decorative figures for private villas and public places throughout the Roman Empire, this copying process caused no disruption – save the effective transference of a champion athlete's original renown to the sculptor who once made his image.

Olympic-style games were organized at Naples and other cities in Italy. It is true, all the same, that actual participation in the Olympic Games came not so much from the western provinces of the Roman Empire as from the East. 'Olympic' festivals were established at such places as Alexandria, Antioch in Syria, Ephesus, Sidon, Smyrna, and Tralles, with one historical source

(John Malalas 10.248, 286) implying that, with imperial permission, the Olympic 'trademark' was franchised abroad by the Eleans. Certainly, inscriptions relating to sporting heroes in these parts show that it was necessary for an athlete who had won at Olympia to specify himself as *Olympionikês Pisaios* – 'victorious in the Pisa Olympics'.

The civic vanity that propelled and was satisfied by such 'international' athletic triumph is apparent in the inscribed statue-base set up during the third century by one inhabitant of Oinoanda, a city in the coastal region of Asia Minor known as Lycia. His name was Euarestos, which itself means 'Mr Well-Approved', and at Oinoanda he was an *agônothetês* – an impresario of games, and probably presiding judge too. *'I have sponsored prizes for the strong in the well-known stadia of brawny Herakles'*, boasts Euarestos, who goes on to say that since he is himself a poet, he has also put up prizes for poetic festivals. He further relates that this is now the fifth set of dedicatory verses he has caused to be engraven in honour of his 'sweet fatherland', because he has already set up no fewer than four statues as 'symbols of virtue and wisdom'. We may presume these were self-portraits, to judge by the concluding message from Euarestos to his fellow-citizens in the market-place of Oinoanda:

Many have endowed cities with fine prizes after their death, but no mortal man while still alive. Only I dared to do so. It gladdens my heart to gaze with delight on the bronze images. Hold back your criticism, all you possessed by monstrous Envy: look on my statue with an eye to follow my example.

(Text in *SEG* XLIV 1182 (B))

In this part of the Roman world, evidently, the institution of formal athletics provided a sign of Greek identity; a statement of cultural affiliation.

The Question of Social Provenance

By the time of this 'agonistic explosion' in the Roman East, it is evident that athletics offered a career path. One writer tells us that an Olympic victor could command an appearance fee of up to five talents, or 30,000 drachmas (Dio Chrysostom, *On Reputation* 11); more significantly, perhaps, inscriptions from Alexandria reveal that local athletes who came back with an Olympic crown were rewarded with immediate rights of citizenship. In the Roman Empire, there is little doubt that athletes used their prowess both to earn a living and to achieve upward social mobility. That athletes could form a professional association or guild is attested by inscriptions – and of course the Neronian club house at Olympia.

Was it always thus? The question has exercised modern scholars so thoroughly that it seems tedious to rehearse its various sub-problems here. The difficulty begins right from the outset, with the information that the first recorded victor of the *stade*-race in 776 BC was Koroibos of Elis, a 'cook'. To what social rank should he be assigned? We have only to remember our own distinctions within the cook/chef category to apprehend that this may not be easy. So it proves, with the Greek *mageiros* indeed translatable as 'cook' – but also used to imply the ritual office of preparing and conducting sacrifice – in which case Koroibos may have been a very important person at Elis.

Greek gymnasia, as we have seen, could be socially exclusive; and it might be argued that excellence in athletics was attainable mainly by those who could devote hours of leisure time to training. But we should not forget that the participation of boys at major meetings gave the opportunity for an athletic 'career' to begin at an early age; and also that for a boy brought up on a farmstead, the gymnasium might have been superfluous. A well-known story in antiquity concerned a farmer's son called Glaukos who won a dramatic victory in the boys' boxing at Olympia *c.*520 BC. Glaukos had once straightened out a ploughshare using his bare fist as a hammer, and this thumping power served him well in the contest: we are specifically told that he was not otherwise skilled at boxing, implying that he had no formal gymnastic training. The farmer's boy subsequently went on to pursue a presumably lucrative career as a prize-winning pugilist (Pausanias 6.10.1–3).

It has been vigorously argued (by David Young) that 'amateurism' is a modern concept, foisted upon antiquity by the wishful thinking of gentlemen-scholars hostile to the very idea of involving money with sport. Pierre de Coubertin, founder of the modern Olympics, tried hard to imagine that ancient athletics were the preserve of high-minded (and well-heeled) aristocrats; the disdain for prize-money is evident, too, in the writings of several twentieth-century 'experts' on Greek and Roman games. They belong to a certain age. When the principles of the English Amateur Athletic Club were first formulated in 1867, they defined an amateur as 'a person who has never competed in an open competition, or for public money ... *or is a mechanic, artisan or labourer*' (italics added), exposing, clearly enough, the sheer social snobbery bound up in this issue.

And there was snobbery in ancient times. Alcibiades is said to have opted for chariot-racing because he did not care to mix with ruffians in the wrestling-ring. Alexander the Great is said to have remarked that he would take part in a running-race only if it were against other kings. Such anecdotes indicate that beyond Olympia's ideology of welcome to all Greeks, nuances of rank and status were not to be ignored. But, of course, they also suggest that outside the hippodrome prince versus ploughboy was a credible bout.

Closedown

The ending of the ancient Olympic festival came about as a result of edicts from Constantinople – the 'new

Rome' established in AD 324 by Constantine the Great, the first Roman emperor to give Christianity official toleration and encouragement. Constantine supported Orthodox or Catholic Christianity, but his Christian successors, influenced by increasingly powerful bishops such as Ambrose of Milan, were not so tolerant of cults they deemed 'pagan' or 'heretical'; nor, eventually, were they much inclined to respect the sort of intellectual freedom enshrined in the philosophical schools of Athens.

It was during the reign of Theodosius I (AD 379–95) that Olympia, along with other long-established Classical sanctuaries, came within the scope of direct prohibition. In AD 380 Theodosius announced Christianity to be the official state religion of the Byzantine Empire. Subsequent edicts from Theodosius in AD 391 and 392 outlawed the practices of sacrifice, libations, garlands, and divination throughout his territory. From recent archaeological work at Olympia it seems that local priests were reluctant to comply, and carried on officiating at least until the interdict was renewed under the rule of Theodosius II (AD 408–50). There is, however, no archaeological evidence that this same Theodosius II had the Temple of Zeus burned down, as chronicles assert, in AD 426. Nor was the statue of Zeus deliberately destroyed. It appears that while Arcadius – son of Theodosius I, father of Theodosius II – was emperor, a dignitary of Constantinople called Lausus made space for the image in his palace, amid other masterpieces of Classical sculpture. Fire, however, devoured the collection.

The ensuing fortunes of Olympia as a site are summarized in Chapter 7. But there is a coda to the Christian closure of Olympia as a religious meeting-place. The Christian hostility towards Olympia was doctrinal: Theodosius I, prompted by bishop Ambrose, was a loyal stalwart of the Nicene Creed, and therefore likely to find all aspects of polytheistic paganism repulsive. However, beyond some strident ecclesiastical complaints about the narcissism and uselessness of athletes – which were not new concerns – and prudishness about nudity, there was nothing in the Christian faith that actively undermined the practice of athletics. The Nietzschean idea that Christianity fostered the *Ressentiment* of 'injured merit' and passive suffering is not supported by early Christian literature and history.

It is well known that the writings of (or those attributed to) the apostle Paul are threaded with the terminology of the *agôn* and the gymnasium. To fight the good fight, to finish the course: these are the strenuous qualifications that will gain 'the crown of righteousness' (II Timothy 4.7). Paul envisaged Christ as the 'forerunner' (Hebrews 6.20) who set an exemplary pace and carried the torch; the Christian vocation was a matter of hard spiritual training to reach a similar sort of self-control (I Corinthians 9. 24–7). So the function of athletic prowess as part of the Greek definition of a hero never faded. On the contrary, it gained fresh currency in the later Roman Empire, when periodic campaigns of persecution against Christian believers were conducted. In the emotive literature of Christian martyrdom, the faithful who provided fatal entertainment in Roman arenas were hailed by Tertullian and Paulinus and other Christian apologists as 'athletes of Christ'. Unlike gladiators, they did not fight for freedom or reprieve. They were volunteers for extreme pain: reminding us, again, that 'athletics' derives from the Greek verb *athleuo* – 'I struggle, I contest; I *suffer*'.

6

OLYMPIA: THE ORIGINS

As we have seen, the conventional date assigned to the first Olympiad of 776 BC was widely perceived as an absolute threshold of Classical chronology. But the Olympic athletic festival cannot have simply sprung into being in 776. What came before?

According to the erudite Roman Varro (writing in the late first century BC), before the first Olympiad was the 'age of fable'; after 776 was history, 'when events [*res gestae*] are contained in truthful chronicles'.

That myths were deemed 'aetiological', betraying the root 'causes' (*aitia*) of things, was a prevalent Classical view. Myths can end in terribly tangled roots, but are nonetheless explanatory of historical development and ritual practices. We shall attempt to follow Olympia's mythical undergrowth as best we can, relating it where possible to the archaeology of the prehistoric

Peloponnese. This calls for a brief priming on the literary sources.

Not only in what follows, but also throughout this book, there are references to ancient writings on Olympia and Greek athletics. It happens that the majority of such writings are in Greek and belong to the second century AD, by which time all Greek-speaking lands were firmly under Roman control, and had been for some time. Lucian, Phlegon, Plutarch, the several generations of writers named Philostratos, and Pausanias – for all that these authors have distinctive voices, they are nevertheless part of the 'Second Sophistic': that is, the flourishing of Greek philosophy and Hellenic culture in the Roman Empire, especially during and after the rule of Hadrian (AD 117–38).

As observed in the previous chapter, Hadrian himself did much to sponsor the proliferation of athletic festivals in the cities of Roman Asia Minor. And Olympia was not neglected. Hadrian's friend Herodes Atticus, who maintained a villa at Eva Kynourias in eastern Arcadia, was a practical benefactor at Olympia and Herodes' wife Regilla once served as Priestess of Demeter, a duty commemorated by the large marble bull that once stood in the semi-circular aquatic niche, or 'Exedra', endowed by Herodes. We also know that a chronicle of Olympic history, covering from 776 BC to AD 140, was compiled by Phlegon of Tralles. That makes another Hadrianic link, for Phlegon was one of the emperor's freed slaves.

But only fragments of Phlegon's text survive. By contrast – as if by recompense – we have the work of his fellow-countryman from Asia Minor, Pausanias.

We have used it often enough so far in this study of the ancient Olympics. Now is the time to admit that the *Periêgêsis tês Hellados*, or 'Guide to Greece', produced by Pausanias not later than *c.* AD 175 is not easy to categorize as a book. A functional guidebook, or the record of a wistful pilgrimage? Its context within the Second Sophistic has encouraged some scholars to treat the work of Pausanias as a largely literary contrivance. The explicit aim of Pausanias was to make a description of 'all things Greek' while Greece was a province of Rome; and there is no doubt that Pausanias exploits Olympia as his showcase *par excellence* for 'all things Greek'. But equally we can accept that Pausanias gives Olympia disproportionate attention – relative to Delphi, or the Athenian Akropolis – because Olympia was indeed *the* primary Panhellenic sanctuary. And what is also clear is that Pausanias knew Olympia well. Just to transcribe the inscriptions on the bases of two hundred or so Olympic victory statues must have occupied him for days, if not weeks.

At one point in his account of the site, Pausanias emphasizes that he personally witnessed what came to light when a Roman senator set about clearing a space for a statue near to the 'Pillar of Oinomaos' (5.20.8). Weapons and harness-pieces were found. Pausanias does not elaborate on archaeological detail. It is enough for him to remind us of his first-hand acquaintance with Olympia. As for the old arms and bridle-bits, it is plain that Pausanias was not surprised. What else was to be expected from a site associated with Oinomaos? Did not the mythology of Olympia say that Oinomaos had been a fierce charioteer?

This expectation requires us to enter the thinking of Pausanias – and plunge faithfully into the age of fable. Here is a story that Pausanias knew about Olympia. And it begins not in the Peloponnese, but on the coast of Asia Minor, close to where Pausanias himself was born, in sight of Mount Sipylos.

The Story of Pelops and Oinomaos

Mount Sipylos rises above old Smyrna, in the Lydian lands mythically ruled by Tantalos. Tantalos was an off-spring of Zeus, but not himself a god. Perhaps he was unhappy as keeper of a kingdom; perhaps he simply tried too hard to ingratiate himself with divine favour. In any case, Tantalos hosted a feast on the peak of Sipylos to which he invited the gods. His guests brought food and took pot luck. Their contributions included nectar and ambrosia; then Tantalos served the stew he had made. He was aware that the Olympian deities were saluted as 'all-knowing'. But would they know what it was they were offered: tender pieces of Pelops – the king's own son?

They would indeed, though not before one of them, Demeter, had gnawed her way through a shoulder-blade.

Throwing the joints back into a cauldron, Rhea, the mother of Zeus, quickly reassembled the boy Pelops, substituting the lost shoulder with one of ivory. Whatever his intentions had been, Tantalos was severely punished. He was consigned in the Underworld to be forever teased ('*tantalized*') – by water he cannot quite reach to drink, and food he cannot quite reach to eat. As for Pelops, amends were made for the butchery at his father's hands. Pelops seemed not only repaired but reborn. His winning looks immediately made him a favourite of the god Poseidon, who gave him some splendid young colts, and chariot-riding skills. On gaining manhood, Pelops set out to travel. He went deep in the land to which he would later give his name – the Peloponnese, or 'Isle of Pelops'. There he found the woman whom he determined should be his wife.

Her name was Hippodameia, which means 'subduer of horses': she could match any man in riding or running. And she was a princess, the daughter of King Oinomaos, who ruled the western margins of Arcadia. But Oinomaos was a dark and difficult man: 'heavy drinker' is what his name implies. There were rumours that his wife Sterope was also his mother; rumours, also, that he loved his daughter Hippodameia too amorously. Oinomaos may have been warned by some oracle that whoever married Hippodameia would be the cause of his death. Certainly he did not intend to let her go. Any man who wanted to take Hippodameia must first prove himself in challenge with the king.

The contest was a chariot-race starting out from the royal city of Pisa, and ending at the altar of Poseidon on the distant Isthmus of Corinth. But this race had a history of not going to the finish. The suitor was allowed to set off first, accompanied by his would-be bride; then Oinomaos gave chase. One main rule applied. If the king caught up with the suitor, it was his right to dispatch the boy by a spear-stab to the back.

With his god-given horses and chariot-handling prowess, Pelops had reason to hope for the best. Oinomaos, however, possessed a team of magical, unbeatable steeds. When young Pelops arrived to make his bid for the princess, a dozen or so young men had already perished in the same attempt. The king kept stark victory-trophies: a set of skulls that bulged above the lintel of his palace. Pelops wavered at the sight: what could he do, but pray to Poseidon for good speed? Yet as he burned for Hippodameia, she burned for him. And Hippodameia had another idea. Her father Oinomaos was proud to make a show of his own experience at handling the reins, but the royal chariot was maintained by its regular driver, called Myrtilos. Hippodameia went secretly to Myrtilos while he prepared the machine for the race. She found him testing the chariot's twin wheels, secured to its axle by two stout cotter-pins of bronze. Hippodameia suggested to Myrtilos that he take out one of these metal pins and substitute it with a replica of wax.

Why – Myrtilos wondered slyly – might he want to scheme against his master? When Hippodameia replied, '*For my sake*', she may not have intended what Myrtilos understood. All that mattered to her then was that Pelops did not join the nodding architrave of losers' heads.

Hippodameia stood by Pelops while the race was mustered. While Pelops took her off in the chariot, the king put a ram to sacrifice. Then he clambered aboard, shaking reins in one hand and a spear in the other. As Oinomaos was gaining hard on Pelops, his chariot lost a wheel and slewed off its course. It was a perfect accident. Oinomaos was thrown, dragged, and trampled to his death.

Pelops was left with double guilt. Though no one much regretted it, there was the death of Oinomaos. Then there was the settlement with Myrtilos, who if menial was nevertheless a son of Hermes. Myrtilos came with Pelops on a journey of purification to the sea. The charioteer grew insistent that Hippodameia had promised him her favours. The two men fought; Pelops hurled Myrtilos into the deep. As Myrtilos went under, he gurgled a curse, calling for doom to fall upon the descendants of Pelops and Hippodameia.

So much is implicit from the petrified tableau of the east pediment of the Temple of Zeus at Olympia, erected *c.*460 BC – not long after Pisa had been attacked and ransacked by predatory Elis. The marble protagonists of the story stiffly present themselves as if on the proscenium of a formal drama: grim Oinomaos, solemn Pelops – and Hippodameia hitching her robes

(Fig. 36). The only expressive figure is a dome-headed seer, holding his hand to his mouth in an exaggerated motion of horror, sharing the plot with viewers below. What we see is overture. These players are poised to enact a primal routine (girl trades father for husband). But more and worse will come as the curse of Myrtilos spills out.

Pelops and Hippodameia produce two sons, Atreus and Thyestes, who dispute their royal inheritance with singular nastiness. The family-eating disorder is revisited when Atreus cuts up his brother's children and serves them at a feast where Thyestes is guest of honour. Aigisthos is the only son of Thyestes to survive, and in due time wreaks revenge within the house of Atreus. But bad things are already happening there, with Agamemnon, the elder son of Atreus, so desperate to lead the Achaean campaign against Troy he would sacrifice his daughter Iphigeneia for the advancement of war. While Agamemnon is at Troy, his wife Clytemnestra takes up with Aigisthos. The pair will murder Agamemnon upon his return; for which it is the turn of Agamemnon's further offspring, Orestes and Electra, to settle the score.

So much by way of summary: enough to note that many painful hours of Classical tragic drama derive their storyline from the result of Pelops' challenge of Oinomaos. For ancient visitors to Olympia this was all common knowledge, and entirely befitting a site of Pan-hellenic status. The communality of the myth did not, however, inhibit its spidery elaborations of detail and

36. Marble ensemble from the east pediment of the Temple of
Zeus at Olympia, *c.*460 BC: Zeus (on larger scale than the other
figures); Pelops; Hippodameia; Oinomaos; Sterope, wife of
Oinomaos; Myrtilos and chariot; Pelops' chariot; two seers,
perhaps Iamos and Klytios, and the personified rivers
Alpheios and Kladeos. Olympia Museum.

gossamer psychology. Even in the brief weave above, we
have had to stitch up and reconcile several narrative
faults, at least one of which goes unnoticed by antique
mythographers (would Myrtilos drive the chariot he had
sabotaged?). But let us say that implausibility, or the
begrudged suspense of disbelief, is a modern demon.
Once there were pilgrims for whom the loose ends of
this story were not troublesome. What mattered to them
was the myth's essential security: its clinging impinge-
ment upon the world.

Those credulous tourists were not disappointed. At

and around and beyond ancient Olympia, paramythic relics and vestiges were substantially in place. Their erstwhile realities may be listed (reference numbers are to Pausanias):

1. In the Altis or sacred precinct of Olympia: the Pelopion – a conspicuous barrow or mound marking the tomb of Pelops (5.13.1–2). His bones were kept separately in a bronze chest (6.22.1); see also items (5) and (6) below.

2. In the nearby Temple of Hera: an ornamental couch that once belonged to Hippodameia (5.20.1). The

Eleans also fetched Hippodameia's bones from the Argolid for storage at Olympia: presumably in the shrine dedicated to her there (6.20.7; 5.22.2).

3. Also in the Altis: a wooden pillar of the palace of Oinomaos – all that was left standing after Zeus blasted the residence with fiery lightning (5.20.6).

4. On display in the Treasury of the Sikyonians at Olympia: the ceremonial dagger of Pelops (6.19.6).

5. Once visible at Olympia, but decayed by the first century AD: the ivory shoulder-blade of Pelops. The bone was already a relic at the time of the Trojan War, when it had been summoned by the Greeks as a necessary aid for victory; it was restored to Olympia only after an eventful journey back, via Delphi (5.13.4–6).

6. In the environs of Olympia, where the city of Pisa once stood: the remains of a sanctuary to Artemis Kordax, marking where Pelops' followers once stomped a boisterous dance, the *kordax*, in thanksgiving to the goddess Artemis: a cult they brought with them from Lydia. The bones of Pelops were kept at a shrine close by (6.22.1).

7. In and around the vicinity of Olympia: various cenotaphs and memorials set up by Pelops – to Myrtilos (6.20.17), to Oinomaos (6.21.3), to the other suitors of Hippodameia (6.21.9–11); also

certain sites associated with the stabling and burial of their horses (for example 6.21.7).

8. At Pheneus, in Arcadia: by the temple of his father Hermes, the tomb of Myrtilos (8.14.10).

9. At Keleai (towards Corinth): displayed upon a rooftop, the chariot of Pelops (2.14.4).

10. Venerated at Chaironeia, in northern Boeotia: the sceptre of Pelops – originally crafted by Hephaistos for Zeus, passed from Pelops to Thyestes and Atreus, subsequently used by Agamemnon (9.40.11).

For Pausanias, these were so many stages on a heritage trail that served to verify a precept laid down by his contemporary, Plutarch. Myths relate to truth as rainbows relate to the sun (*De Iside* 358F): wondrous as they may seem, myths are the phenomena of history's atmosphere. For the Greeks, myths might be written up, dramatized, recited, and parodied; but ultimately, and originally, myths *happened*.

At our modern distance from all this, we are naturally tempted to rationalize the realities of the paramythic sights/sites that Pausanias describes. Consider the scapula of Pelops – a divine piece of prosthetic surgery, which after the heroization of Pelops travelled to Troy, was lost at sea, fished up, and eventually restored to Olympia. We are earnestly informed that age-worn mammalian bone *can* have the appearance of ivory. And it is quite plausible that ancient Greeks came upon the fossil remains of prehistoric mastodons (large, elephant-like mammals), and took them as the skeletons of heroic colossoi (for the shoulder-blade of Pelops, the species *Mammuthus primigenius* is suggested).

In a similar spirit of sceptical reasoning, it has been suggested that the 'Pillar of Oinomaos' was some antique phallic stone, the focus of some Mycenaean 'pillar-cult' – or, perhaps, the turning-post of an *Ur*-Stadium that may have projected westwards into the area later marked off as the Altis.

Yet only one item from the above list of relics has so far been located – the Pelopion. Excavations in the Altis have duly investigated its antiquity. From 1879 to 1906, two distinguished German archaeologists, Adolf Furtwängler and Wilhelm Dörpfeld, battled over the question of whether Olympia was active as a cult site during the so-called 'Mycenaean Age': the period *c.*1600–1200 BC when fortified settlements flourished in various parts of the Peloponnese, including cities celebrated in the epics of Homer – Pylos, Tiryns, Argos, and of course 'well-walled Mycenae' itself. Dörpfeld was convinced that Olympia must have had a Mycenaean existence, and the Pelopion offered him the main chance of proving it. But Furtwängler, working through the objects found in the early strata of votive activity at Olympia, pointed to the conspicuous absence of any Mycenaean pottery or other artefacts among these finds.

The stakes of this debate were high. It was a compatriot of Dörpfeld and Furtwängler, Heinrich Schliemann, who two decades previously had claimed to have found the grave of Agamemnon – Pelops' grandson – at Mycenae. Would the Pelopion yield a similar satisfaction?

It transpires that the mound of the Pelopion indeed marks a burial, and a very old one. Of all the man-made structures in the Altis, the Pelopion is by far the most ancient. But it is too old to fit with Dörpfeld's theory of a Mycenaean Olympia. The only burial found (that of a child) was said be of the Neolithic period; but more recent examination of the mound, and its surrounding kerb, have shown that it belongs to the Early Bronze Age of the third millennium BC (more precisely, the period known as 'Early Helladic II'). True, the earthwork itself had not been left intact since then – it yielded, for instance, the boasting-stone of Bybon (see p. 63), among many other archaic offerings – and there were also traces of human habitation around the Pelopion dating to the late third millennium ('Early Helladic III'), dwellings whose outlines may have inspired the apsidal shape of the sixth century BC Council House at Olympia. But those in pursuit of an historical Pelops – complete with a Bronze-Age grave comparable to those at Mycenae – have been conclusively thwarted.

In fact the Pelopion, though poetically saluted by Pindar as the 'tomb' of Pelops (*Olympian* 1.94), was not strictly reckoned as such in antiquity. Pausanias explicitly says that an ossuary existed elsewhere. The monumental demarcation of the tumulus as a cult space was not effected until the early fourth century BC, when a pentagonal walled enclosure was put up. The sole act of sacrifice there, according to Pausanias, was that of a black ram, conducted in a pit rather than at an altar. By defining these honours, Pausanias makes it clear that as Zeus was paramount among the gods worshipped at Olympia, so Pelops was the hero of the site. To what extent, therefore, should we seek the origins of the Olympic Games in the myth and cult of Pelops?

Myth, Ritual, and the 'Invention of Tradition'

Pelops is mentioned just once in the poems of Homer, as an ancestral holder of regalia inherited by Agamemnon. A single epithet summarizes his reputation: Pelops is *plêxippos*, 'lasher of horses' (*Iliad* 2. 104). Immediately we recall the chariot-race with Oinomaos; and we may wonder if that contest were not some symbolic precedent for chariot-racing – historically the most important and prestigious event of the ancient Olympics. (An awareness of the story was apparently kept vivid in the Hippodrome at Olympia, where an olden mound projecting on one side of the course was said to be haunted by either Myrtilos, or Oinomaos, or one of the dead suitors; some malevolent spirit, at any rate, which caused horses to panic as they passed by the spot, and was therefore called 'horse-frightener', *taraxippos*: Pausanias 6.20.15.)

For all the mythical, archaeological, and icono-graphical importance of Pelops at Olympia, however, Pausanias does not specify the hero as a cause or progenitor of institutional games. Hippodameia, by contrast, is explicitly connected with the all-female games, or 'Heraia' (see p. 120). As Pausanias relates (5.16.2), Hippodameia choreographed sixteen maidens to celebrate her marriage to Pelops with dancing and contests in honour of Hera. Since the Pelops–Oinomaos contest was chosen for depiction on the Temple of Zeus, and also figured upon an archaic carved wooden box kept in the Temple of Hera (the 'Chest of Kypselos': see Pausanias 5.17.7), we may accept that it did seem to ancient vistors like some prototypical tournament akin to athletic effort. But it is hardly a straight race – either Oinomaos or Pelops has an unfair advantage (on the Chest of Kypselos, Pelops evidently wins the race thanks to Poseidon's winged horses); or else Pelops resorts to bribery and cheating. And how would a mythical char-iot-race account for all the other events of the Olympic Games – not least a short-distance foot-race, tradition-ally considered to be the first instituted contest at Olympia?

These problems of evidence and aetiology have not deterred some scholars from trying to analyse the Pelops story as if it contained clues to finding an original ritual-istic structure for the Olympic Games. Perhaps the most ingenious attempt came from F. M. Cornford, who published his arguments as a chapter of Jane Harrison's adventurous 1912 study of Greek religion, *Themis*. Harrison herself was the most committed of the several so-called 'Cambridge Ritualists' who believed that myths arose from 'primitive' rites: both she and Cornford were much influenced by J. G. Frazer, whose anthropological explanation of one minor custom of Classical religion grew into thirteen volumes of *The Golden Bough*.

Cornford – his theory deriving from undergraduate lectures on Pindar's epinikian odes – was comprehensive in his approach. Not only was the chariot-race between Pelops and Oinomaos significant of a bid for kingship, symbolically re-enacted whenever young men competed for the 'crown' of athletic victory. For Cornford, the entire Olympic festival was founded upon cults of vegetation and fertility; and all elements of the Pelops myth, including the young hero's dismembering and reassemblage on Mount Sipylos, belonged to a pattern of initiation, death, and resurrection.

Cornford's hypothesis was hotly contested. William Ridgeway, Professor of Archaeology at Cambridge, insisted on an alternative explanation. At the funerals of heroes (or 'ancient worthies', as Ridgeway liked to call them), games were customarily staged – as described, for example, in Book 23 of Homer's *Iliad*. Ridgeway believed that Greek tragedy had evolved out of the dramatic lamentations that once took place at heroic funerals. He proposed the same origin for Greek athletics: the *epitaphios agôn*, or 'contest by a tomb'.

There is a good deal of comparative anthropological evidence that might be cited to bolster this proposal. Funerary games, whether intended to propitiate the spirit of the deceased, or determine a successor to the dead man by tests of courage, strength, and speed, can be cited from pre-modern societies around the world. In 1941 the Swiss scholar Karl Meuli drew some persuasive ethnographic comparisons between funerary customs of certain nomadic Asian tribes and the early Olympic programme. Extensions of this approach which seek the generic origins of sport in rites of hunting or male initiation remain speculative. But Meuli's case is supported by the nature of early votive offerings at Olympia, which so abundantly suggest a site frequented by people whose pastoral livelihoods were invested in cattle and horses – as characterized for 'the coming of the Dorians' to these parts *c.*1000 BC.

Further variations of this hypothesis for an origin of the Olympic Games in funerary ritual have been advanced, notably by Ludwig Drees and Hans-Volkmar Herrmann. But the essential difficulty with these explanations abides in the archaeological reality of an empty grave – a Pelopion without Pelops. Francis Cornford was no archaeologist; nonetheless his conceptual understanding of the nature of Greek hero-cults was acute. Faced with both literary and archaeological evidence for the heroization of Pelops at Olympia, we do well to invoke Cornford's statement that for the purposes of cult activity, the typical Greek hero 'is not a dead man with a known name and history commemorated by funeral games. His title stands not for a personality, but for an office, defined by its functions and capable of being filled by a series of representatives.' In other words, the tales and supposed relics of Pelops may define or characterize the role of Olympia's hero; yet it is the existence of the hero-cult which requires Pelops, not vice versa.

Olympia is not an island. The archaeology of the Pelopion can be explained by reference to the wider pattern of hero-worship elsewhere in the Greek world, especially across the Peloponnese. During the period of 750–650 BC, it is apparent that inhabitants of landscapes marked by tombs of bygone ages undertook acts of formal reverence at those tombs. Offerings were deposited in and around the graves, prompted by motives we can only surmise. It was after *c.*750 BC that the Ionian epics credited to Homer began to circulate on the Greek mainland: the enchantment of this poetry was doubtless heightened by finding visible, tangible locations for characters who were larger than life and truly 'awesome'. We know that shrines were raised to Agamemnon and Menelaos in the late eighth century, near Mycenae and Sparta respectively (though not by tombs); it may have been enough simply to have denoted a Bronze-Age grave as the burial-place of an unknown 'hero', providing people in its vicinity with a right of agrarian occupation, perhaps, or staking a political boundary.

We have seen how the site of Olympia was historically disturbed by proprietorial struggles between various Peloponnesian city-states. Its early establishment as a sacred haunt must have been similarly subject to rival claims to possession; and the rivals would come armed with their own justifications of myth and cult.

This process helps to explain the plurality of myth ical traditions at Olympia. To describe the range and nuances of the mythology associated with Olympia would be exhausting. But suppose we resume with Pausanias, and match his account with the basic ancient understanding of a first Olympiad in the early eighth century BC (that is, 776). By Varro's reckoning, as we have noted, 'history' began after 776, and was preceded by the age of fable. In turn, the age of fable was preceded by another period, prior to the 'cataclysm' of global inundation ('before the Flood') – a time when everything was 'bedimmed' (*adêlos*, as the Greeks termed it). According to this threefold epochal division, Olympia's mythology could be summarized as follows:

[1] *Pre-Cataclysm: 'The Age of Obscurity'.* A shrine at Olympia is raised to Kronos, son of Ouranos ('the heavens') and Gaia ('the earth'), who married his sister Rhea. Kronos devoured and then later regurgitated his offspring – but one of them, Zeus, was entrusted by Rhea to five primal guardians, called Dactyls ('Fingers') or Kourêtes ('Lads'), on Mount Ida in Crete. One of

these guardians was called Herakles: he had races with his brothers at Olympia, and set the custom of crowning the winner with a wreath of wild olive. The Olympian deities (so called because of their permanent residence on Mount Olympus in northern Greece) also had wrestling, running, and jumping contests at Olympia.

[2] *Post-Cataclysm: 'The Age of Fable'.* Cretan descendants of 'Idaean Herakles' reclaimed Olympia as a meeting-place for games. One local king was Endymion, the mortal loved by the Moon: he offered his throne to whichever of his sons could run fastest (and Endymion's tomb, according to Pausanias, was to be located in the Stadium, near the starting-mark: 6.20.9). Then came Pelops, who after his victory over Oinomaos staged games in honour of Zeus. Two generations later, a great-grandson of Pelops arrived – Herakles.

A pause is needed here, before bewilderment descends. The multiplication of the name of Herakles caused confusion in antiquity (see Cicero, *On the Nature of the Gods* 3.42), and the modern reader is hardly helped by the second Herakles here being distinguished in Pausanias as 'son of Amphitryon' when most of his associated mythology – including the 'Labours' – rely on the understanding that this Herakles was fathered (albeit furtively) by Zeus.

Further confusion arises from the mixed identity of the post-cataclysmic Herakles as both a Panhellenic and Peloponnesian hero. Reference has already been made (p. 173) to the 'Dorian' occupation of the Peloponnese in

the late second millennium BC. We have also noted how
the metopes on the Temple of Zeus set out a sequence of
vignettes illustrating ideal athletic virtue by his *dodekathlon* (p. 73). Here we should also mention that one strand
of Greek mythology made the Dorian invaders 'descendants of Herakles' (*Herakleidai*) who were staging a
heroic return to the area, assisted by Oxylos, who
became a king of Elis; and further, that one of the
Labours depicted, the 'Cleansing of the Augean Stables'
was given particular Olympic resonance by those
mythographers who named Augeas as an earlier king of
Elis. Augeas was a chieftain whose standards of animal
care were so slovenly that his sheds of several thousand
cattle had not been mucked-out for decades: so the
only way that Herakles could get them clean was to
divert the course of the Alpheios. The temple relief
shows Athena prodding her staff at a likely conduit
(Fig. 37).

Only a decade or two before that scene was carved,
Pindar hailed Herakles as instigator of the cult of Zeus
at Olympia, and founder of the Olympic Games as part
of that cult (*Olympian* 10.42–59). The occasion, as
Pindar defines it, was indeed to celebrate victory in the
task of purging the Augean stables. It was Herakles who
named the Hill of Kronos, pegged out the Altis, con-
secrated the site, and formulated the contests. Pindar
knew the story of Pelops and Oinomaos; he may even
have been aware of Herakles the Idaean Dactyl; but perhaps because he sang for his patrons 'a Dorian refrain'

37. Herakles cleansing the Augean Stables: marble relief from the Temple of Zeus at Olympia, *c.*460 BC.

(*Olympian* 3.5), he preferred Herakles as Olympia's creator . Though this version of Olympic myth was not 'canonical' for Pausanias, it was treated as orthodoxy by other writers. (Beyond the opening claims of the

'Olympic Discourse' by Lysias, see also Apollodorus 2.7 and Diodorus Siculus 4.14.)

The story of the Heraklean creation of the Olympic festival was amplified – thus Polybius (12.26) makes Herakles the first enforcer of the Olympic Truce – and, for all its fabulous context, seriously 'accepted'. A fragment of Plutarch, for instance, relates how the mathematician and philosopher Pythagoras calculated the physical dimensions of Herakles using the 'fact' that Herakles had measured out the stadium at Olympia with 600 units of his footsteps (other stadia were also 600 feet, but shorter in length: therefore, a proportional ratio should reveal how tall Herakles stood by comparison with ordinary men: Sandbach Fr. 7; see also Aulus Gellius, *Attic Nights* 1.1).

Coeval with Herakles were Castor and Pollux, the *Dioskouroi* or 'Heavenly Twins', who competed at Olympia. Then, says Pausanias (5.8.5), the Games lapsed – until their revival by Iphitos, a king of Elis.

[3] *776 and thereafter: 'The Historic Olympics'*. As noted by Pausanias, the associations made between Iphitos and the 'Olympic Truce' were marked by a statue, inside the Temple of Zeus, of Truce crowning Iphitos (5.10.10); and, on display in the Temple of Hera, 'the discus of Iphitos', inscribed with the traditional proclamation of peace for the duration of the Games. Phlegon also knew that Iphitos, along with Lycurgus of Sparta and a certain Cleosthenes, had re-established the contests at Olympia with a view to spreading peace –

homonoia – around the Peloponnese (*FrGrH* 257 F1). But Iphitos remains a shadowy figure, and Pausanias is careful to stress that 'revival' under Iphitos was more like reinvention, since the athletic programme had fallen into virtual oblivion. Accordingly, the first Olympiad of 776 featured just one event, the one-way sprint (*dromos*) won by Koroibos of Elis; and it was not until the 14th Olympiad that the two-length foot-race (*diaulos*) was added, with the longer distance race (*dolichos*), pent-athlon, and wrestling, boxing, and other contests coming at later intervals. Chariot-racing began 'historically' only in the 25th Olympiad (680 BC), and events for boys were not introduced until the 37th (632 BC).

What are we to make of all this? It is routine, and obligatory, to observe that the boundaries between 'myth' and 'history' were often blurred in ancient Greek thinking. (It was F. M. Cornford who showed how even the scrupulously 'investigative' historian Thucydides tended to be *mythistoricus* – a writer who shaped his narratives upon mythical structures.) In the course of this book, we have allowed anecdotes of 'actual' ancient athletes, such as Milo of Croton, to be flavoured with elements of fable. So it is no surprise to find the ancient accounts of Olympia's origins steeped in essentially fabulous concoctions. A few voices may be heard from antiquity urging scepticism – the early first-century AD topographer Strabo is one, warning us not to believe tales told about early Olympia (*Geographia* 8.3.30–1) – but these can safely be counted as a minority. Likewise, abstract theories about some primal purpose of sport were not seriously considered. When Plutarch wonders if Olympia did not start off with a simple duel of one-to-one combat, the idea is shrugged off as a sign of drunken incoherence (*Sympotic Questions* 675c). For Pausanias and most other visitors to Olympia, the sanctuary's mythology was sufficient to explain its complex, dogmatic, and 'time-honoured' protocols.

Such ancient levels of credence need not deter us, however, from at least establishing reasons for the development and elaboration of this mythology. And the most obvious factor here is 'the invention of tradition'.

Modern historians, led by Eric Hobsbawm, have taken some delight in demonstrating that many ceremonies we believe to be dignified by great age are, in fact, relatively recent fabrications. Flags, anthems, costumes, pageants, and jubilees – they may define the nations of today, but their semblance of folkloristic antiquity is just that: a semblance. Traditions, the ways of doing things in the past, provide charters or sanctions for ways of doing things in the present; so if customs change, then traditions must change too. We shall see, in the following chapter, how the modern Olympic movement has spawned its own spuriously antique traditions, such as the torch-relay of an eternal 'Olympic flame' – introduced for the Berlin Olympics of 1936. It may be some comfort, then, to conclude that the origins of the Olympic festival as reported to and by Pausanias in the time of Marcus Aurelius were surely likewise: the accumulation of legend and liturgy at a place of prehistoric settlement which began to be developed as a monumental sanctuary in the eighth century BC.

The Archaeology of Cult at Olympia

Most of the great sites of ancient Greece were sanctuaries, and most of them became 'great' in the course of a continuous development beginning in what is often termed the 'Geometric' period, the eighth century. On the Athenian Akropolis, there appears to have been no sacred architecture until *c.*700 BC. On Delos, and at Delphi, Eleusis and the Argive Heraion, evidence of cult activity prior to the eighth century – including Mycenaean traces – is either non-existent or inconspicuous.

It is tempting to fit Olympia into this scheme. But with Olympia it is necessary to speak of a *monumental* development beginning in the eighth century, because the earliest votive dedications made at the site probably belong to the eleventh or tenth century BC. A sequence of 'prite' bronze tripods seems to begin in the early ninth century. And although some of these tripods appear to be imports from further afield, the archaeological record suggests that in its earliest phase as a sanctuary (*c.*1000–750 BC), Olympia was no more than an occasional meeting-place frequented by local inhabitants – people from early Iron-Age settlements in a proto-Elean territory bounded by the rivers Peneios and Alpheios.

'Early Iron Age' or 'Protogeometric' – however we refer to this period, the dating of its structures and artefacts is notoriously difficult. What happened between the 'collapse of the Mycenaean world' c.1200 BC and the 'rise of the Greek *polis*' c.750 BC is a topic for which the phrase 'the Dark Age of Greece' may still be appropriate. But there is no doubt among archaeologists on two chronological points: that the quantity of votives deposited at Olympia increases quite spectacularly in the eighth century; and that at around the same time, the practice begins of sinking temporary well-shafts at Olympia, indicative of the necessity to provide water for periodic influxes of visitors.

Jewellery, weapons, and tripods are among the numerous offerings recovered from the Altis area; but above all, Olympia's archaic strata were found packed with thousands of figurines. In bronze or terracotta, these mostly present miniature models of quadrupeds, with a number of riders and charioteers too (**Fig. 38**). The likelihood is that temporary workshops were set up at Olympia to produce these objects (some of them look decidedly like 'rejects'), and therefore that votives were supplied to worshippers *in situ*.

Later on, of course, sculptors working on a larger scale would be present at the established Olympic athletic festival, to take commissions for victory monuments. But what kind of festival was it, c.750 BC?

38. 'Charioteer' bronze votive figurine from the Altis, of the 'Geometric period' *c*.800–750 BC.

Following Homeric prescription, we have accepted that the tripods dedicated in the Altis and Stadium areas were symbolic of victory in some athletic contest. If the first tripods were dedicated at Olympia not long after *c*.1000 BC, then we should suppose the first trials of athletic prowess to have taken place then. The miniature votive chariot-groups may also testify to two-horse chariot-racing at Olympia as early as *c*.800 BC. But from the archaeological evidence there is no reason to think that the formal, four-yearly 'Olympics' began in the year 776. One of the site's most assiduous modern excavators, Alfred Mallwitz, went to his grave (in 1986) with the firm conviction that 'the Games were not founded before the last quarter of the eighth century'. Mallwitz picked on a date of 704 BC as the most likely year of the First Olympiad. Any proposed 'absolute' beginning, however, must remain nominal. Long before Pausanias, the genesis of the Olympic Games was mythologized. The archaeology of Olympia at least testifies that such ancient 'received wisdom' was not entirely fantastic. If not in 776 precisely, then it was during the eighth century BC that the rustic sanctuary at Olympia began to host large numbers of pilgrims attracted to its numinous seclusion. However fictitious the archaic parts of the victory-lists may be, it remains true that athletes from the west-central Peloponnese predominate – consistent with a picture of local frequentation at the site. And if not the full quadrennial programme of athletic events, the ritual features were already in place that elevated sporting competition as a mode of cult observance.

Agricultural thanksgiving; rites of fertility and vegetation; a tournament for stock-breeders and herdsmen – the votive dedications at Olympia up to and including the eighth century indicate the general nature of the gathering. Compared to the high number of animal figurines – Furtwängler in 1879 reported digging them up at the rate of 700 per week – only small quantities of pottery have been recovered, which may mean that eating and drinking were not significant elements of worship here. Among the earliest identifiable deities worshipped at Olympia are several goddesses strongly associated with crops and productivity – Hera, Demeter, Eileithyia (a birth goddess), Gaia (Mother Earth), and Themis (another 'Mother Earth' figure, who also developed attributes of prophecy and presidence over mortal assemblies). The first monumental temple at Olympia was that dedicated to Hera in the late seventh century BC. And circumstantial historical evidence suggests that the original formal meetings at Olympia took place annually, not every four years.

So when did the cult of Zeus become paramount here; and how did athletic competition establish itself as a direct, primary mode of worshipping Zeus? Bluntly, the answer is that we do not know. We cannot even say when the site of Olympia gained its name, presumably in honour of Zeus Olympios. All that can be said may be summarized as follows.

By the mid-eighth century BC, Olympia was a site already sacrosanct to local people over many decades – though without formal temple structures, nor any established facilities for regulated athletic contests. During the eighth century, there was a marked increase in numbers of worshippers at this site, generating interest, status, and revenues for the sanctuary. As part of the sanctuary's development, elementary challenges of speed and physical prowess were gradually incorporated into a periodic celebration of Zeus and other Olympian deities. However these athletic challenges came about, they soon gained a religious, social, and political significance far beyond Olympia itself. By the late sixth century BC, 'the Olympic Games' were institutionalized at Olympia, paradigmatic of honour to Zeus at large, and a meeting, point for Greeks and Greek city-states across the Mediterranean. The origins of this extraordinary development were obscure even then. And so it was all mythologized.

7

OLYMPIA: THE AFTERLIFE

E arly in the morning we crossed a shallow brook, and commenced our survey of the spot before us with a degree of expectation from which our disappointment on finding it almost naked received a considerable addition. The ruin, which we had seen in evening, we found to be the walls of the cell of a very large temple, standing many feet high and well-built, its stones all injured ... From a massive capital remaining it was collected that the edifice had been of the Doric order. At a distance before it was a deep hollow, with stagnant water and brick-work, where, it is imagined, was the Stadium. Round about are scattered remnants of brick-buildings, and the vestiges of stone walls. The site is by the road-side, in a green valley, between two ranges of even summits, pleasantly wooded ...

So Olympia was officially 'rediscovered' by Richard Chandler, an Oxford don, in 1766. The note of anti-climax rings through Chandler's report to the London-based Society of Dilettanti, which had sponsored the expedition. Olympia should have been a more revelatory find than this. Led by a Turkish scout, Chandler had made an irksome journey through fields of cotton-shrubs, thistles, and liquorice, only to find a stagnating pool of half-tumbled pillars and walls; a stone robbed desolation that was home to clouds of gnats.

Of course the site was not absolutely unknown. Local peasants were aware of it – not so much as a source of marble and brick, but rather more useful for the spits of iron or lead that had served as dowels inside the column drums, pieces of metal that could be extracted, if the columns were toppled. Long ago, earthquakes had assisted in the toppling; followed by inundation by the Kladeos, and then floods from the course of the Alpheios, which washed away the Hippodrome. These natural events took place not long after c. AD 500. Then, historically speaking, the entire Peloponnese devolved into a sort of backwater existence. During the thirteenth century, a band of Frankish Crusaders found it relatively easy to set up feudal rule across the land mass, which they named *le Morée*, or Morea, on account of a pervasive tree – the mulberry. Byzantine delegates, Ottoman Turks, and Venetian adventurers then alter-nated as overlords, with the Ottomans prevailing to establish a *Turkokratia* lasting until Greece gained independence in 1821. A Venetian map of the Morea made in the mid-sixteenth century suggests that the name of the site of Olympia had half-survived (possibly as *Noglimcchi*, in transcription) – but it was 'lost' to wider European awareness.

Some knowledge of ancient athletics was preserved through the Middle Ages in Europe by medical experts, dependent as they were upon the writings of Galen, one-time emergency surgeon to gladiators at Pergamon in Asia Minor, subsequently doctor to the Roman emperor Marcus Aurelius in the second century. Galen's copious tracts and treatises contained sporadic (if often disparaging) allusions to the regimes of exercise and diet laid down by earlier Greek sources. Then came the numerous textual citations of Olympia and athletics arising in the Classical literature being studied and edited by European humanist scholars in the fifteenth century. The first specialist dissertation based on such literary sources was composed (in Latin) by a French scholar, Pierre du Faur, or 'Petrus Faber', and published at Lyons in 1592 under the title *Agonisticon, sive de re athletica* etc., 'On Athletic Matters'. This collected the information made explicit about ancient practice in, for example, the odes of Pindar, and tried valiantly to square it with precepts of muscular Catholicism. As yet there was little archaeological knowledge of ancient athletics, and such Roman copies of epinikian statues as came to light were simply listed as 'nude torsos'.

How far a general knowledge of Olympia and the

Olympic Games had extended beyond scholarly circles in early eighteenth-century Europe is marked by a melodrama scripted by a prolific Italian librettist at Vienna, Father Pietro Metastasio, in 1733. Put to music by Vivaldi, Metastasio's *Olympiad* does not enjoy great popularity today, though its plot is sufficiently lurid for any opera-goer's taste. It is effectively an ancient Greek version of the Turandot story. Based on a tale in Herodotus (6.126–31: in turn surely indebted to the Pelops–Oinomaos myth), the plot relates how Kleisthenes, the tyrant of Sikyon, wished to match his daughter in marriage to a worthy young man. Himself a victor in the Olympic chariot-race, he announced the challenge on the banks of the Alpheios at Olympia. The suitors duly applied, and were put to various tests, some sporting. (In Herodotus, a promising contender disqualifies himself by not only dancing on the dinner-table of his potential father-in-law, but doing a headstand and kicking his legs in the air.) Eventually Kleisthenes' daughter is won by an Athenian, Megakles – also a chariot-victor at Olympia.

Metastasio's work travelled beyond the ambience of Viennese opera-houses. One enthusiastic translator of the drama in the late eighteenth century was Rigas Pheraios-Velestinlis, a Thessalian activist for Greek independence who saw the value of ancient Olympia as a rallying-point for modern Hellenic patriots. But still the actual site of Olympia lay unexplored – though the desirability of investigation was made plain enough first by the French antiquarian Abbé Montfaucon (in 1723), and the Rome-based German *doyen* of ancient art, J. J. Winckelmann (1717–68).

Winckelmann's appreciation of the 'perfect' boyish bodies of Greek athletes as revealed in Roman marbles tends to be viewed nowadays as an expression of his own homoerotic interests. Whatever his motives, Winckelmann had high hopes – based on his reading of Classical sources, especially Pausanias – that Olympia should yield thousands of 'young and manly figures . . . wonderworks of art by the thousand'. He never lived to realize his dream of obtaining a permit to excavate from Turkish authorities. Sundry European travellers reached the site in the late eighteenth and early nineteenth centuries, some making sketches and plans of what could be seen: but no actual excavation occurred until 1829, when savants attached to the French military uncovered part of the Temple of Zeus and the little Christian basilica built over the 'Workshop of Pheidias'. A few of the relief sculptures from the temple were disinterred: they are now to be found in the Louvre in Paris.

It is probably a testament to Winckelmann's posthumous influence that the implementation of a full-scale archaeological project at Olympia eventually devolved to his fellow-countrymen. In particular it was Ernst Curtius, a Classical scholar who (as court-appointed private tutor) had influence over German royalty. Curtius saw Olympia as a young man in 1838; by 1853 he had submitted a formal proposal for its excavation. He shared Winckelmann's belief that the site held many treasures; he also considered it nothing less than Christian duty to redeem them.

The urgency of this mission was absorbed by many diplomatic manoeuvres. Curtius also faced solid reluctance on the part of Bismarck, Germany's first chancellor, to commit Reich funds to the scheme. For a while it seemed that the great buccaneer of Classical archaeology, the privately funded and virtually lawless Heinrich Schliemann, might usurp the project. Then at last official excavations began in October 1875. Unlike Schliemann's raids on Troy and Mycenae, these were systematic, well-documented campaigns. With only a few missing structures, the sanctuary was revealed to be very much as Pausanias had promised – at least in its layout. The bumper harvest of statues did not material-ize. But the quantity of finds in other respects – such as the mass of votive figurines sorted and classified by Adolf Furtwängler – was gratifying; while such sculptural *Meisterwerke* as the Nike of Paionios and the 'Hermes of Praxiteles', and the pedimental pieces from the Temple of Zeus, exemplary of the so-called 'Strong' or 'Severe' style, kept connoisseurs of Greek art happy.

'Germany has exhumed what remains of Olympia. Why should not France be able to reconstitute its splendours?' That question came from a minor French aristocrat, Baron Pierre de Coubertin. As the German excavations were brought to a provisional end (in 1881), Coubertin was preoccupied not so much with the salvage of antique

Greek statuary as the moulding of new young citizens in France and the wider world. His model for 'the athletic education' (*la pédagogie sportive*) was not drawn from the ancient world, rather the British public-school system as he had studied it during the 1880s. It was not with Homer but a copy of *Tom Brown's Schooldays* at his elbow that Coubertin conceived his dream of an Olympic renaissance. Tom Brown was a fictitious boy, but it was no secret where his schooldays took place: at Rugby, the institution whose purpose, as stated in 1828 by its incoming headmaster Thomas Arnold, was to produce 'Christian men'. At Rugby, Arnold inculcated, as Coubertin saw it, the virtues of 'initiative, daring, decision, and the habits of self-reliance and blaming no one but oneself when one stumbles' through a system of punishing physical exertion.

France did not leap to accept the Anglophile educational paradigm offered by Coubertin. He turned his energies towards realizing a more grandiose dream. What if Arnold's ideal of breeding 'gentlemanly conduct' were internationalized – through the renewing and adapting of the ancient Greek Olympic Games?

Coubertin's proposal was not entirely bold. In various countries, certain sporting and commercial festivals had already claimed the title 'Olympic'. Some rustic jamborees in the west of England had been doing so since the seventeenth century. The Greeks had staged national revivals in 1859 and 1870. But Coubertin's global vision, matched by his tireless disposition to evangelize abroad, outshone all previous efforts. At an 'International Congress of Amateurs' summoned to Paris in 1894, Coubertin raised his glass to 'the Olympic idea, which has traversed the mists of the ages like an all-powerful ray of sunlight and returned to illumine the threshold of the twentieth century with a gleam of joyous hope'.

Coubertin was not himself a champion athlete, but he might have scored well in florid oratory at ancient Olympia. His flair, energy, and influence were largely responsible for the first modern Olympics being held at Athens in 1896, with an almost authentically antique venue provided by the Panathenaic Stadium – originally laid out in the fourth century BC, embellished with marble by Hadrian in the second century AD, and hurriedly restored for 1896. Coubertin's Norman baronial lineage and his traditional Catholic faith combined to ensure, however, that these 'revived' Olympics were very much his own creation – a sporting synod of gentlemen-amateurs, more invested with the values of Medieval chivalry than Classical renown. Thirteen nations took part in the 1896 Games, which were financed, organized, and mostly won by the hosts. The social pedigree of the foreign competitors was as Coubertin imagined it should be: from the United States, therefore, only Ivy League types, travelling to Athens first-class with an entourage of flunkeys; from Britain, a cohort of Oxford- and Cambridge-educated men who were horrified when it transpired that their team also included some minor

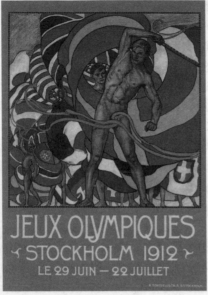

39. Poster for the Stockholm Olympics, 1912.

staff from the British Embassy at Athens who aspired to enter the cycling race.

The history of these modern Olympics is well documented elsewhere: it is another story. Our account of ancient Olympia's afterlife, however, is not quite at an end. The German excavations of 1875–81 were conducted and published very efficiently. But there was still more scope for work at the site: in particular, one massive task remained – the digging of the Stadium. The occasion of the modern Olympics being staged by Germany in 1936 offered archaeologists an opportunity to press their case. Otto von Bismarck had always been suspicious of their high-minded and expensive plans. His National Socialist counterpart was much more receptive.

Hitler's dispensation secured 50,000 Reichsmarks as an annual subsidy for another six-year campaign. The Führer gave his personal blessing to the resumption of German excavations at Olympia, 'which for more than a thousand years was the site of festivals expressing the religious feelings and the basic convictions of the Greek *Volk*' (a sentiment reported in the Nazi newspaper, *Völkischer Beobachter*, 3 August 1936). An exhibition at Berlin themed around 'Sports of the Greeks' was curated by two distinguished Classical archaeologists, Theodor Wiegand and Carl Blümel. But it was Dr Carl Diem, the mastermind of logistics for the eleventh modern Olympiad, who devised a more ingenious way of relating Olympia past to Olympism present. In July 1936, white-robed figures gathered reverently at a brazier set up in the Altis. A flame, kindled in the Stadium from rays of the sun, was brought to light the fire. A torch was dipped into the fire. Then a runner picked up the torch, and set off on the first leg of a 3,000-kilometre relay that would carry the 'Olympic flame' all the way (via Athens) to Berlin. This brand new tradition formed the opening sequences of an epic film about the Berlin Olympics made by Leni Riefenstahl – commissioned, again, with Hitler's warm support (**Fig. 40**).

Hitler accepted that the next Olympics were already assigned to Tokyo. Thereafter, he intended, they should return to Germany for good. So as the archaeologists

40. Lighting the torch at Olympia: still from Leni Riefenstahl's *Olympia*, 1936.

began clearing masses of silt from the Stadium at Olympia, Hitler and his chief architect Albert Speer set about designing a 400,000-capacity *Reichssportfeld* at Nuremberg. It was to be the permanent centre for racially pure 'Pan-Aryan' Olympiads.

Before that could happen, of course, it was necessary to go to war – with the shooting.

EPILOGUE

The excavation of Olympia remains a project of central significance to Classical history and archaeology. But curiosity about retrieving information about ancient athletics extends far beyond academia. It is no exaggeration to claim that the values of physical culture articulated in Classical Greece have conquered the modern world. The revived Olympics have played some part in that; though the main power belongs to mass advertising, cinema celebrity cults, and the commercial packaging of leisure, 'well-being', and personal appearance.

The rapport between antiquity and the present in this respect is worth pursuing. The international phenomenon of bodybuilding, for instance, is relatively recent in its technical development, yet directly indebted to the Classical past. Eugen Sandow, founder of *Sandow's Magazine of Physical Culture* in 1898 and often hailed as the 'father' of bodybuilding, was moved to transform himself into a professional strongman after seeing Classical statues on display in Italian museums. Similar inspiration was later also acknowledged by the influential 'Charles Atlas' (born Angelo Siciliano). Of all the bodybuilding books, magazines, and correspondence courses that proliferated in the early twentieth century, there were few that did not capitalize upon the resonance of Classical tags for masculine strength and beauty ('Achilles', 'Apollo', 'Adonis', and so on) or else deploy some rippling Classical marble as their leading man (none more pumped-up than the so-called 'Farnese Hercules', a Roman bath-house piece derived from the work of Lysippos). And when Alan Calvert, the pioneer of adjustable weightlifting equipment in 1902, came to give his Philadelphia-based firm a name – what else should it be but the Milo Barbell Company?

This book has endeavoured to locate the legendary Milo in a certain social and historical setting; it is presented as a serious study. But an ultimate truth may now be conceded. Sport – even serious sport – is *fun*.

To chase a ball around a field is fun; to plough a field is not fun. Fun is diversion: an escape from the necessities of work and survival. Allowing sport to keep its essence of fun, we may also like to remind ourselves where Olympia is situated. Olympia lies on the fringes of Arcadia – that mountainous area of the central Peloponnese idealized in European tradition as the semi-mythical home of pastoral ease and 'escapism'; a byword for nymphs and shepherds at play in an enclave of shameless simplicity. In Classical credence, Arcadia was the stamping-ground of the goat-god Pan. Even today, Arcadia preserves some sense of its remote and verdant reputation. The traveller still finds beehives stood above every glen, old ladies filling their aprons with wild salad, and goats roaming the roadside. One of the villages here – not very far to the east of Olympia – has the curious name of Pothos, which means 'longing', or 'desire'. It is tempting to seize a symbolic significance to the name. Is this the gateway to Arcadia – our yearning for the Golden Age of rustic, childish innocence?

Geographically, Olympia occupies a place on Arcadia's edge; spiritually, Olympia may be claimed to belong dead centre – in that wished-for haven where we live for the sake of amusing ourselves. This is a deeply peaceful place; where, if we strive, it is to show ourselves at our best.

SOURCES AND
FURTHER READING

Since the various works of J. H. Krause, notably *Die Gymnastik und Agonistik der Hellenen* (Leipzig, 1841), the literature on Olympia and Greek athletics has grown enormous. Confronted by such a quantity of reading matter on the practice of physical effort, one simple reaction might be, '*Just do it* . . .' And a new contributor can only plead to enter the lists with the hope of offering a slightly more delicate synthesis than a host of predecessors. The bibliography offered here is necessarily selective, and structured thematically to the sequence of foregoing chapters.

To begin with, however, some general debts and recommendations. M. Golden, *Sport and Society in Ancient Greece* (Cambridge, 1998) presents a lively introduction to the subject – with an equally lively bibliographic essay. H. A. Harris, *Greek Athletes and Athletics* (London, 1964) remains useful despite its anachronistic enthusiasm for amateurism in ancient sport. W. Raschke (ed.), *The Archaeology of the Olympics* (Wisconsin, 1988) collects a set of essays ranging beyond Olympia, but including a valuable summary by Alfred Mallwitz to complement his handbook, *Olympia und seine Bauten* (Munich, 1972). J. Swaddling, *The Ancient Olympic Games* (London, 1980) is a succinct account mainly illustrated from the collections of the British Museum.

There is no substitute for first-hand knowledge of the site. Beyond the contribution of Mallwitz, one should include solid summaries by Ludwig Drees (translated as *Olympia: Gods, Artists, and Athletes* (London/New York, 1968)) and H.-V. Hermann, *Olympia: Heiligtum und Wettkampfstätte* (Munich, 1972). The current director of the German mission, Ulrich Sinn, has also produced a valuable monograph: *Olympia: Kult, Sport und Fest in der Antike* (2nd edn., Munich, 2002); translated as *Olympia: Cult, Sport, and Ancient Festival* (Princeton, 2000).

Periodically there are exhibitions of artefacts relating to ancient athletics: one catalogue that remains useful is D. Vanhove (ed.), *Le Sport dans la Grèce antique: Du Jeu à la Compétition* (Brussels, 1992). See also A. La Regina (ed.), *Nike: il gioco e la vittoria* (Rome, 2003).

For the distilled praise of ancient epigraphic testimonies to athletes, Luigi Moretti's *Iscrizioni agonistiche greche* (Rome, 1953) provides a very representative sample.

There are notable papers in W. Coulson and H. Kyrieleis (eds.), *Proceedings of an International Symposium on the Olympic Games* (Athens, 1992).

At the time of writing, proceedings of the Sydney 2000 conference entitled *Sport and Festival in the Ancient Greek World*, edited by D. Phillips and D. Pritchard, were not yet published; however, thanks to one of the contributors (John Davidson) I have included some anticipatory references to the volume.

1 'War Minus the Shooting'

The application of George Orwell's phrase to Olympia is not new: see P. Cartledge in P. E. Easterling and J. V. Muir (eds.), *Greek Religion and Society* (Cambridge, 1985), pp. 103–15. Orwell's original essay, published in the *Tribune* (December 1945) may be found in Volume 4 of his *Collected Essays,*

Journalism and Letters, edited by S. Orwell and I. Angus (Harmondsworth, 1970), pp. 61–4.

'THE AGONISTIC SPIRIT': Jacob Burckhardt's argument, first published in Volume IV of his *Griechische Kulturgeschichte* (Berlin/Stuttgart, 1889), may be found in an abridged translation edited by Oswyn Murray, entitled *The Greeks and Greek Civilization* (London, 1998), pp. 160–213. On Burckhardt's 'Hegelianism', see E. H. Gombrich, *Ideals and Idols* (Oxford, 1979), pp. 24–59. Nietzsche's most emphatic statement on the matter comes in an essay entitled 'Homer's Wettkampf' – see G. Colli and M. Martinari (eds.), *Friedrich Nietzsche: Nachgelassene Schriften 1870–1873* (Berlin, 1973), pp. 277–86; excerpted and translated as 'Homer's Contest' in W. Kaufmann (ed.), *The Portable Nietzsche* (New York, 1954), pp. 32–9. My mention of Nietzsche's debt to Burckhardt is not a charge of plagiarism: that Nietzsche was intrigued by the topic of Greek competitiveness is already evident in his detailed work on the text of the poetic duel between Homer and Hesiod – 'Der Florentinischer Traktat über Homer und Hesiod, ihr Geschlecht und ihren Wettkampf', and *Certamen quod dicitur Homeri et Hesiodi*, published respectively in *Rheinisches Museum für Philologie*, vols. 25 (1870), pp. 528–40 and 28 (1878), pp. 211–49; also collected in F. Bornmann and M. Carpitella (eds.), *F. Nietzsche: Philologische Schriften (1867–1873)* (Berlin, 1982), pp. 270–364. See also V. Ehrenberg, 'Das Agonale', in his *Ost und West: Studien zur geschichtlichen Problematik der Antike* (Brünn, 1935), pp. 63–96; J. Huizinga, *Homo Ludens* [1938] (London, 1970), pp. 91–6; and I. Weiler, '*Aien aristeuein*. Ideologiekritische Bemerkungen zu einem vielzitierten Homerwort', in *Stadion* 1.2 (1976), pp. 200–27.

The case of Sparta is exceptional – and somewhat neglected in my text, despite the pervasive influence of Sparta upon

Olympia over centuries. For an analysis, see S. Hodkinson, 'An Agonistic Culture? Athletic Competition in Archaic and Classical Spartan Society', in S. Hodkinson and A. Powell (eds.), *Sparta: New Perspectives* (London, 1999), pp. 147–87.

CRITIQUE OF ATHLETICS: Plutarch, *Life of Philopoemen* 3 clearly states the strategic disparagement of athletics as military preparation (other Greek commanders accredited with similar views include Agesilaos of Sparta and the Peloponnesian general Epaminondas). That such disparagement became a commonplace for Roman orators and writers is indicated by the sources cited in the commentary on Juvenal 3.68 by J. E. B. Mayor, *Thirteen Satires of Juvenal*, Vol. 1 (London, 1880), p. 189. An obvious bias is evident in the overt hostility towards the emperor Nero and his support of Greek and Greek-style athletics (for example, Tacitus, *Annals* 14.20.4).

2. In Training for Beautiful Goodness

On gymnasia generally, see J. Delorme, *Gymnasion* (Paris, 1960). On their architecture, the Roman Vitruvius remains the best source: *De architectura* 5.11. The gymnasium complex at Olympia (including the *palaistra*) is analysed in C. Wacker, *Das Gymnasion in Olympia: Geschichte und Funktion* (Würzburg, 1996). Further aspects of social history are explored in N. Fisher, 'Gymnasia and the democratic values of leisure', in P. Cartledge, P. Millett, and S. von Reden (eds.), *Kosmos: Essays in Order, Conflict and Community in Classical Athens* (Cambridge, 1998), pp. 84–104. The inscribed gymnasiarchal rubric from Beroia is fully published and expounded in P. Gauthier and M. B. Hatzopoulos, *La loi gymasiarchique de Beroia* (Athens, 1993).

Valuable essays on social history: T. Scanlan, *Eros and Greek Athletics* (Oxford, 2002).

On the sculpted ideal: A. F. Stewart, *Art, Desire and the Body in Ancient Greece* (Cambridge, 1996), with review essay by N. J. Spivey, 'Meditations on a Greek Torso', in *Cambridge Archaeological Journal* 7.2 (1997), pp. 309–14.

The best edition of Philostratos remains that of Julius Jüthner, *Philostratos Über Gymnastik* (Amsterdam, 1969 [Leipzig 1909]).

3. The Programme of Agony

On the Olympic oath: M. Lämmer, 'The Nature and Significance of the Olympic Oath in Greek Antiquity', in D. P. Panagiotopoulos (ed.), *The Institution of the Olympic Games* (Athens, 1993), pp. 141–8.

In the list of Olympic victors recorded by the Oxyrhynchus papyrus (see p. 134), the mule chariot race is repeatedly omitted, and the following order of events given as standard for the fifth century BC: *stadion, diaulos, dolichos, pentathlon, palê, pyx, pankration, paidôn stadion, paidôn palê, paidôn pyx, hoplitês, tethrippon, kelês.* Hugh Lee has recently reviewed the entire procedure of the Games: see H. M. Lee, *The Program and Schedule of the Ancient Olympic Games* (*Nikephoros* Supplement 6: Hildesheim, 2001).

The significance of the body-type exhibited by the Motya charioteer is explored by M. Bell, 'The Motya Charioteer and Pindar's Isthmian 2', in *Memoirs of the American Academy in Rome* 40 (1995), pp. 1–30. On the conduct of the 'heavy events', see M. B. Poliakoff, *Combat Sports in the Ancient World* (Yale, New Haven, Conn., 1987). Some technical aspects of wrestling statue groups are noted in E. Künzl, *Frühhellenistische Gruppen* (Cologne, 1968).

The problems surrounding the pentathlon are summarized in D. G. Kyle, 'Winning and Watching the Greek Pentathlon', in *The Journal of Sport History* 17.3 (1990), pp. 291–305; see also G. Waddell, 'The Greek Pentathlon', in *Greek Vases in the J. Paul Getty Museum* 5 (1991), pp. 99–106.

GAMES FOR GIRLS: A comprehensive essay on female running in ancient Greece, by P. A. Bernadini, is to be found in P. A. Bernadini (ed.), *Lo Sport in Grecia* (Bari, 1988), pp. 153–84; see also M. Dillon, 'Did Parthenoi Attend the Olympic Games? Girls and Women Competing, Spectating, and Carrying Out Cult Roles at Greek Religious Festivals', in *Hermes* 128 (2000), pp. 457–80; and (for a partisan account) A. C. Reese and I. Vallera-Rickerson, *Athletries: The Untold History of Ancient Greek Women Athletes* (Costa Mesa, 2003).

4. Sweet Victory

IDENTIFYING THE WINNERS: Fundamental for tracing the names and identities of Olympic victors is Luigi Moretti's *Olympionikai: I vincitori negli antichi agoni olimpici* (Rome, 1957), with addenda from the same author published in *Klio* 52 (1970), pp. 295–303, and in Coulson and Kyrieleis, pp. 119–28. H.-V. Herrmann, 'Die Siegerstatuen von Olympia', in *Nikephoros* 1 (1988), pp. 11–83 gives a thorough analysis of statues recorded by Pausanias.

PREMIUM OF VICTORY: On the importance of victors in city-state politics: C. Mann, *Athlet und Polis im archaischen und frühklassichen Griechenland* (Göttingen, 2001). Heraldic announcements: N. B. Crowther, 'The Role of Heralds and Trumpeters at Greek Athletic Festivals', in *Nikephoros* 7 (1994), pp. 135–55. Defining *kudos* in the sixth and fifth centuries BC: L. Kurke, 'The Economy of Kudos', in C. Dougherty and L. Kurke (eds.), *Cultural Poetics in Archaic Greece* (Cambridge, 1993), pp. 131–63. The Archilochos fragment: D. E. Gerber, *Greek Iambic Poetry* (Harvard, 1995), pp. 283–7. On Panathenaic prizes and their values, see D. G. Kyle, 'Gifts and Glory', in J. Neils (ed.), *Worshipping Athena* (Wisconsin, 1996), pp. 106–36; and by the same, 'Games, Prizes and Athletics in Greek Sports', in *Classical Bulletin* 74 (1998), pp. 120–5. Exainetos of Akragas: Diodorus Siculus 13.82.8–7.

CHRONOLOGY OF THE OLYMPIADS: Doubts about the victory-list of Hippias are elegantly presented by J. P. Mahaffy, 'On the Authenticity of the Olympic Register', in *The Journal of Hellenic Studies* 2 (1881), pp. 164–78; see also B. Peiser, 'The Crime of Hippias of Elis. Zur Kontroverse um die Olym-pionikenliste', in *Stadion* 16.1 (1990), pp. 37–65. On the Oxyrhynchus citation, see B. P. Grenfell and A. S. Hunt, *The Oxyrhynchus Papyri*, Part II (London, 1899), pp. 85–95. *Olympionikai* of Eratosthenes of Cyrene: *FrGrH* 241 F14.

EPINIKIAN POETRY: A good introduction to the genre is given in D. A. Campbell, *The Golden Lyre* (London, 1983), pp. 54–83; also in Maurice Bowra's *Pindar* (Oxford, 1964), pp. 159–91. Charles Segal's summary of Pindaric epinikian comes in his *Aglaia* (Lanham, 1998), p. 3. For detailed read-ings, see M. R. Lefkowitz, *The Victory Ode* (New Jersey, 1976); D. E. Gerber, *Pindar's Olympian One: A Commentary* (Toronto, 1982); and M. M. Willcock, *Pindar: Victory Odes* (Cambridge, 1995). The latter volume gives analysis of Pindar's *Olympians* 2, 7, and 11: most of the other *Olympians* have dedicated commentaries, but an excellent overall edition is collected by Luigi Lehnus, *Pindaro: Olimpiche* (Milan,

1989). I quote from B. L. Gildersleeve, *Pindar: The Olympian and Pythian Odes* (Amsterdam, 1965 [1885]), p. xxxvi. On the 'effortless' epinikian for Alcibiades: C. M. Bowra, 'Euripides' Epinician for Alcibiades', in *Historia* 9 (1960), pp. 68–79. On the infusion of Pindar's epinikian with heroic values, see G. Nagy, *Pindar's Homer* (John Hopkins, 1990). I have said little about the actual nature of the performance of an epinikian ode: it is explored in W. Mullen, *CHOREIA: Pindar and Dance* (Princeton, 1982), pp. 3–20. On the uneasy rapport between Pindar and the sculptors, see P. O'Sullivan, 'Victory Song, Victory Statue: Pindar's Agonistic Imagery and its Legacy', in *Sport and Festival*.

EPINIKIAN STATUARY: W. W. Hyde, *Olympic Victor Monuments and Greek Athletic Art* (Washington, 1921) remains valuable. On the epigrams of victory statues: J. Ebert (ed.), *Griechische Epigramme auf Sieger an gymnischen und hippischen Agonen* (Leipzig, 1972). The interplay of poetry and statues is analysed in D. Steiner, *Images in Mind* (Princeton, 2001), pp. 259–65 (with remarks too on athletic eroticism, pp. 222–34). On the making of bronzes: C. Mattusch, *Classical Bronzes* (Cornell, 1996); and by the same author, *The Victorious Youth* (Los Angeles, 1997) – a handy monograph on the 'Getty athlete' (Fig. 33). On Polykleitos: N. J. Spivey, *Understanding Greek Sculpture* (London, 1996), pp. 36–43; P. Amandry, 'A propos de Polyclète: Statues d'Olympioniques et carrière de sculpteurs', in K. Schauenburg (ed.), *Charites* (Bonn, 1957), pp. 63–87; H. Beck *et al.* (eds.), *Polyklet: Der Bildhauer der griechischen Klassik* (Frankfurt, 1990); A. H. Borbein, 'Polykleitos', in O. Palagia and J. J. Pollitt (eds.), *Personal Styles in Greek Sculpture* (Cambridge, 1996), pp. 66–90; W. Moon (ed.), *Polykleitos, the Doryphoros and Tradition* (Wisconsin, 1995); and M. Marvin, 'Roman Sculptural Reproductions or

Polykleitos: The Sequel', in A. Hughes and E. Ranfft (eds.), *Sculpture and its Reproductions* (London, 1997), pp. 7–28. On Milo's statue: E. Ghisellini, 'La statua di Milone di Crotone', in *Xenia* 16 (1988), 43–52. The accumulation of Greek victory-images in the Roman marble repertoire is carefully catalogued in F. Rausa, *L'immagine del vincitore* (Treviso/Rome, 1994). For the fragments of bronze originals found at Olympia, see P. C. Bol, *Grossplastik aus Bronze in Olympia* (*Olympische Forschungen* 9: Berlin, 1978).

HEROIZATION OF ATHLETES: F. Bohringer, 'Cultes d'athlètes en Grèce classique: propos politiques, discours mythiques', in *Revue des Etudes Anciennes* 81 (1979), pp. 5–18; B. Currie, 'Euthymos of Locri: A Case Study in Heroization in the Classical Period', in *Journal of Hellenic Studies* 122 (2002), pp. 24–44.

PARAMOUNTCY OF WINNING: Some qualifications to the view taken here: see N. B. Crowther, 'Second-Place Finishes and Lower in Greek Athletics', in *Zeitschrift für Papyrologie und Epigraphie* 90 (1992), pp. 97–102. On the satiric gibes at hopeless athletes attributed to Lucillius, see L. Robert, 'Les épigrammes satiriques de Lucillius sur les athlètes. Parodie et réalités', in *L'épigramme grecque* (*Entretiens sur l'antiquité classique* 14, Geneva, 1969), pp. 181–295. The inscription relating to Marcus Aurelius Asclepiades is also discussed by Robert (who unveiled very many inscriptions relating to ancient athletics): see L. Robert, *Hellenica* 7 (1949), pp. 105–13.

5. The Politics of Contest

A shrewd synthesis of political vicissitudes is to be found in E. N. Gardiner, *Olympia* (Oxford, 1925), pp. 77–174.

PHASE I: There is little here that is not more fully discussed in A. Hönle, *Olympia in der Politik der griechischen Staatenwelt* (Bebenhausen, 1972).

PHASE II: For Olympia's contribution to an ideology of Panhellenism, see J. M. Hall, *Hellenicity* (Chicago, 2002), pp. 154–68. On the 'Olympic Truce': M. Lämmer, 'Der sogennante olympische Friede in der griechischen Antike', in *Stadion* 8/9 (1982/3), pp. 47–83.

PHASE III: On the pattern of *euergetism*, or 'doing good', at Olympia, see H. W. Pleket, 'Olympic Benefactors', in *Zeitschrift für Papyrologie und Epigraphik* 20 (1976), pp. 1–18. For Hadrian's promotion of athletic festivals in the cities of the eastern Mediterranean: M. T. Boatwright, *Hadrian and the Cities of the Roman Empire* (Princeton, 2000), pp. 94–104; O. van Nijf, 'Local Heroes: Athletic Festivals and Elite Self-Fashioning in the Roman East', in S. Goldhill (ed.), *Being Greek under Rome* (Cambridge, 2001), pp. 306–34.

THE QUESTION OF SOCIAL PROVENANCE: Still the standard essay on this topic is H. W. Pleket, 'Zur Soziologie des antiken Sports', in *Mededelingen van het Nederlands Instituut te Rome* 36 (1974), pp. 57–87; for Pleket's (mostly unrepentant) afterthoughts, see Couslon and Kyrielis, pp. 147–52. The sentiment that the ancient Olympics (and Classical athletics generally) declined into 'pot-hunting' recurs in the works of twentieth-century British Classicist Harris (himself a keen but mediocre cricket-player) and Gardiner ('the Nemesis of success in athletics is professionalism, which is the death of true sport'): see E. N. Gardiner, *Athletics of the Ancient World* (Oxford, 1930), pp. 99–116. That this sentiment has a bogus justification from Classical antiquity is surely proven: see

D. C. Young, *The Olympic Myth of Greek Amateur Athletics* (Chicago, 1984).

The snobbery of Alcibiades was defended by his son, in Isocrates, *On the Team of Horses*, 33–4.

CLOSEDOWN: V. C. Pfitzner, *Paul and the Agon Motif: Traditional Athletic Imagery in the Pauline Literature* (Leiden, 1967) not only analyses Paul's apostolic use of athletic metaphors, but collects the comparanda in Hellenistic and Roman philosophy – for example Epictetus, *Discourses* 1.24; Marcus Aurelius, *Meditations* 3.4.

6. Olympia: The Origins

PAUSANIAS: The writer contriving an 'imaginative geography': J. Elsner, 'Structuring "Greece": Pausanias' *Periegesis* as a Literary Construct', in S. Alcock, J. Cherry, and J. Elsner (eds.), *Pausanias: Travels and Memory in Roman Greece* (Oxford, 2001), pp. 3–20. Pausanias the diligent observer at Olympia: C. Habicht, *Pausanias' Guide To Ancient Greece* (California, 1985), pp. 149–51.

PELOPS AND OINOMAOS: The subtleties of the story are analysed by J. Davidson in his contribution to *Sport and Festival*; for the twists and tangles of the Tantalos/Pelops myth, see T. Gantz, *Early Greek Mythology* (John Hopkins, 1993), pp. 531–45. That Pindar in his *Olympian* 1 sought to create a mythology suitable to match the fifth-century BC prestige of chariot-racing is argued by Gregory Nagy in his *Pindar's Homer* (Baltimore, 1990), pp. 116–35. On the archaeology of the Pelops myth, see H.-V. Herrmann, 'Pelops in Olympia', in *Stele: Festschrift Nikolaos Kontoleon* (Athens, 1980), pp. 59–74. The skeletal *realia* of Pelops' remains are discussed in A. Mayor, *The First Fossil Hunters* (Princeton, 2001), pp. 104–10.

THE GAMES AS AN 'ENACTMENT' OF SEASONAL RITES: F. M. Cornford, 'The Origin of the Olympic Games', in J. Harrison, *Themis* (Cambridge, 1912), pp. 212–59: the heated debate over Cornford's ideas, involving not only William Ridgeway but also A. B. Cook and J. G. Frazer, is recorded in the *Cambridge Review* during 1911 (numbers of 16 and 23 February, and 9 March).

ALTERNATIVE EXPLANATIONS: Karl Meuli's theory appeared as 'Der Ursprung der Olympischen Spiele', in *Der Antike* 17 (1941), pp. 189–208; further ethnographical comparisons made in K. Meuli, *Der griechische Agon* (Cologne, 1968). See also L. Drees, *Der Ursprung der Olympischen Spiele* (Schorndorf, 1974); H.-V. Herrmann, 'Zür ältesten Geschichte von Olympia', in *Athenischen Mitteilungen* 77 (1962), pp. 3–34; D. Sansone, *Greek Athletics and the Genesis of Sport* (Berkeley, 1988); and much else surveyed in I. Weiler and C. Ulf, 'Der Ursprung der antiken olympischen Spiele in der Forschung. Versuch eines kritischen Kommentars', in *Stadion* 6 (1980), pp. 1–38. On the early dedications at Olympia: C. Morgan, *Athletes and Oracles* (Cambridge, 1990), especially pp. 30–9; H. Kyrieleis, 'Neue Ausgrabungen in Olympia', in *Antike Welt* (1990), pp. 177–88. My allusion to the conviction of Mallwitz regarding dates comes from *Olympia-Bericht* XI (Berlin, 1999), p. 199; also argued in his contribution to W. Raschke *op. cit.*, pp. 79–109.

7. Olympia: The Afterlife

Discovery of the site: R. Chandler, *Travels in Greece* (Oxford, 1776), pp. 294–5.

Much varied material on Olympia's *Nachleben* is to be found in M. Zerbini's curiously titled *Alle fonti del doping* (Rome, 2001). On Winckelmann, Curtius, and the story of Olympia's excavations, see H.-V. Herrmann, 'Die Ausgrabungen von Olympia. Idee und Wirklichkeit', in *Stadion* 6 (1980); and S. L. Marchand, *Down From Olympus: Archaeology and Philhellenism in Germany, 1750–1970* (Princeton, 1996), pp. 77–91.

ATHENS 1896: To the accounts of R. Mandell, *The First Modern Olympics* (Berkeley, 1976) and J. J. MacAloon, *This Great Symbol: Pierre de Coubertin and the Origins of the Modern Olympic Games* (Chicago, 1981), important correctives are added by David Young in Coulson and Kyrieleis, pp. 175–84; see also D. C. Young, 'Origins of the Modern Olympics', in *International Journal of the History of Sport* 4 (1987), pp. 271–300; *idem*, *The Modern Olympics: A Struggle for Revival* (John Hopkins, 1996).

BERLIN 1936: R. D. Mandell, *The Nazi Olympics* (Illinois, 1987); H. J. Teichler, 'Coubertin und das dritte Reich', in *Sportwissenschaft* 3 (1981), pp. 361–78.

Epilogue

D. Chapman, *Sandow the Magnificent: Eugen Sandow and the Beginnings of Bodybuilding* (Illinois, 1994).

INDEX

Figures in *italics* refer to illustrations.